Anti-discri...

UNIVERSITY OF
GLOUCESTERSHIRE
at Cheltenham and Gloucester

...selling Practice

FRANCIS CLOSE HALL
LEARNING CENTRE
Swindon Road Cheltenham
Gloucestershire GL50 4AZ
Telephone: 01242 714600

PROFESSIONAL SKILLS FOR COUNSELLORS

The *Professional Skills for Counsellors* series, edited by Colin Feltham, covers the practical, technical and professional skills and knowledge which trainee and practising counsellors need to improve their competence in key areas of therapeutic practice.

Titles in the series include:

Counselling by Telephone
Maxine Rosenfield

Medical and Psychiatric Issues for Counsellors
Brian Daines, Linda Gask and Tim Usherwood

Time-limited Counselling
Colin Feltham

Personal and Professional Development for Counsellors
Paul Wilkins

Client Assessment
edited by Stephen Palmer and Gladeana McMahon

Counselling, Psychotherapy and the Law
Peter Jenkins

Contracts in Counselling
edited by Charlotte Sills

Counselling Difficult Clients
Kingsley Norton and Gill McGauley

Learning and Writing in Counselling
Mhairi MacMillan and Dot Clark

Long-term Counselling
Geraldine Shipton and Eileen Smith

Referral and Termination Issues for Counsellors
Anne Leigh

Counselling and Psychotherapy in Private Practice
Roger Thistle

The Management of Counselling and Psychotherapy Agencies
Colin Lago and Duncan Kitchin

Group Counselling
Keith Tudor

Understanding the Counselling Relationship
edited by Colin Feltham

Practitioner Research in Counselling
John McLeod

Anti-discriminatory Counselling Practice

Edited by
Colin Lago
and
Barbara Smith

SAGE Publications
Los Angeles • London • New Delhi • Singapore

SAGE Publications Ltd
1 Oliver's Yard
55 City Road
London EC1Y 1SP

SAGE Publications Inc
2455 Teller Road
Thousand Oaks, California 91320

SAGE Publications India Pvt Ltd.
B1/I1 Mohan Cooperative Industrial Area
Mathura Road, New Delhi 110 044
India

SAGE Publications Asia-Pacific Pte Ltd
33 Pekin Street #02-01
Far East Square
Singapore 048763

British Library Cataloguing in Publication data
A catalogue record for this book is available from the British Library

Library of Congress Control Number: 2002107100

ISBN: 978-0-7619-6646-3 (hbk)
ISBN: 978-0-7619-6647-0 (pbk)

Typeset by C & M Digitals Pvt Ltd., Chennai, India
Printed and bound in Great Britain by
Athenaeum Press Ltd., Gateshead, Tyne & Wear

Contents

About the Authors   vii

Foreword   xi
Natalie Rogers

Acknowledgements   xv

1   Ethical Practice and Best Practice   1
Colin Lago and Barbara Smith

2   Anti-racist Counselling Practice   16
Oye Agoro

3   Developing Anti-disabling Counselling Practice   33
Mairian Corker

4   Gay Affirmative Practice   50
Graham Perlman

5   Woman-centred Practice – Two Perspectives   62
    (i)   The rhythm model
Jocelyn Chaplin

    (ii)   A radical feminist therapy perspective   68
Bonnie Burstow

6   Child-centred Counselling Practice   75
Barbara Smith and Mark Widdowson

7   Counselling Older Adults   87
Ann Orbach

8   Counselling and Religion   99
Nick J. Banks

9   Class and Counselling   109
     Anne Kearney

10   Double, Triple, Multiple Jeopardy   120
     Roy Moodley

11   Oppression and Pedagogy: Anti-oppressive
     Practice in the Education of Therapists   135
     Barbara Smith and Keith Tudor

Index   151

About the Authors

Oye Agoro was born in the UK, of West African ancestry. She holds a BA in Sociology and Social Anthropology from the University of Hull. She trained as an Intercultural Psychotherapist with Nafsiyat/University College, London. During the 1990s she worked for eight years as a social action psychotherapist with The Forward Project, a black mental health resource in West London. Currently she is Director of The Lorrimore, a voluntary sector agency providing a range of integrated mental health services in Southwark and Lambeth. Oye is an accredited member of the British Association for Counselling and Psychotherapy.

Nick Banks PhD is a Chartered Clinical Psychologist and Senior Lecturer in Counselling at the University of Nottingham, UK. He acts as an expert witness in court proceedings with children and families and has a particular interest in abuse, neglect, adoption and fostering and a specialist interest in black identity issues.

Bonnie Burstow is an academic, a radical feminist psychotherapist and an anti-racist and anti-psychiatry activist. Having taught full time in the social work departments at Carleton University and the University of Manitoba, she is currently cross appointed between the graduate adult education program and the graduate counselling psychology program at the Ontario Institute for Studies in Education at the University of Toronto. Burstow is best known for such works as *Radical Feminist Therapy: Working in the Context of Violence*, Sage, 1992; *Shrink-Resistant: The Struggle Against Psychiatry in Canada*, New Star 1988; and *Ethischer Kodex Fiministischer Thaerapie* (trans: The Ethics of Feminist Therapy), in *Statt Psychiatrie*, Peter Lehmann (ed.), Berlin Peter Lewhmann Antipsychiatrieverlag, 1993.

Jocelyn Chaplin is a feminist psychotherapist/counsellor who has been in private practice for 20 years. She is the author of many publications including *Feminist Counselling in Action*, Sage (1998) and *Love in an Age of Uncertainty*, Harper Collins (1993). Jocelyn co-founded the Serpent Institute in 1989. This was a training organization for counselling and psychotherapy using humanistic and psychodynamic approaches within a framework of goddess spirituality and feminist understandings. She has facilitated workshops and training courses for women at the Women's Therapy Centre, Hammersmith Council, Camden Institute and many others, including the Mediterranean island of Gozo. Visiting ancient sites sacred to the goddess, painting and writing about them, has also been an important part of her work. Jocelyn has been involved in community work and women's groups in Hammersmith and Shepherds Bush in London where she lives and works.

Mairian Corker is currently a visiting Senior Research Fellow at Kings College London, where she is researching discriminatory language and disability from a discourse analytical perspective. Among the first deaf people to qualify as a counsellor in mainstream counselling training, she was involved in counselling and advising parents of deaf children whilst working as Education Officer for the National Deaf Children's Society. She then worked for a number of years in community practice with deaf, deafened and hard of hearing adults, and taught on the counselling skills certificate course for deaf people at Westminster Pastoral Foundation. Mairian is author of numerous interdisciplinary publications, which include *Counselling – The Deaf Challenge* (1994) and *Deaf Transitions* (1996) (both published by Jessica Kingsley), and is an Executive Editor of the leading disabilities studies journal *Disability & Society*.

Anne Kearney is a freelance trainer, supervisor, counsellor and author working in Manchester having taught adults for many years. Her writing includes *Counselling, Class & Politics – Undeclared Influences in Therapy*, PCCS Books (1996). Anne's interests are in politics and working with diversity. She is a founder member of The Counselling Collective.

Colin Lago is Director of the Counselling Service at the University of Sheffield. Initially trained as an engineer, Colin went on to become a full time youth worker in London and then a teacher in Jamaica. Since qualifying as a counsellor in his early thirties he has worked as a counsellor in higher education for more than two decades. He was chair and executive committee member of the Association for Student Counselling and was a founder member and co-chair of the RACE Committee of the British Association for Counselling and Psychotherapy. He is an Accredited Counsellor and Fellow of BACP and a Registered Practitioner with UKRC. Deeply committed to transcultural concerns, he has had articles, videos and books published including: *Race, Culture and Counselling* (with Joyce Thompson), *The Management of Counselling & Psychotherapy Agencies* (with Duncan Kitchin), *On Listening and Learning: Student Counselling in Further and Higher Education* (with Geraldine Shipton), and *Experiences in Relatedness: Group Work and the Person Centred Approach* (co-edited with Mhairi Macmillan). A further co-edited book is planned, *On Anger and Hurt – Exploring Issues in Multicultural Counselling* (with Roy Moodley).

Roy Moodley is Assistant Professor in the Counselling Psychology Programme at Ontario Institute for Studies in Education of the University of Toronto. He was formerly Assistant Director for Research and Development at Thomas Danby College, Leeds and received his PhD in psychotherapy from the Centre for Psychotherapeutic Studies, University of Sheffield. He has published papers on race, counselling and psychotherapy, masculinity and management and access to higher education.

Ann Orbach comes from a background of occupational therapy in psychiatric hospitals as well as freelance journalism on mental health subjects. After qualifying with the Guild of Psychotherapists and gaining membership, she worked for 25 years as a psychotherpist in private practice, as well as supervising and training counsellors. She recently helped set up SAGE (Senior Age) Counselling Service for older people in West Sussex and East Hampshire. Her publications include *Not Too Late: Psychotherapy and Ageing* and *Life, Psychotherapy and Death* (Jessica Kingsley Publishers). She is now retired, but still writing.

Graham Perlman works in transactional analysis psychotherapy in South London in a private practice for gay men and is an Associate Therapist of Pink Therapy Services, as well as training in personal development skills. He lives with HIV and his current interests include the transference implications of gay identity and HIV in the therapeutic relationship and holistic perspectives on well-being. He has written on Transactional Analysis and gay issues.

Barbara Smith is a UKCP-registered psychotherapist working as a Lecturer in Counselling and Social Work in Liverpool. She also has a private psychotherapy practice, specializing in Transactional Analysis with adults and children in individual and group psychotherapy. She has a strong research interest in anti-discrimination and anti-oppression. She has worked on 'Adventure Therapy' programmes with women with troubled eating and is involved in research and publishing in these areas. She works extensively with survivors of childhood sexual abuse having previously been a child protection social worker. She is a supervisor and trainer for counsellors and social workers working with children.

Keith Tudor is a qualified social worker and a qualified and registered psychotherapist with the UKCP both as a humanistic psychotherpist and as a group psychotherapist and facilitator. He is in private/independent practice as a therapist, supervisor and trainer in Sheffield where he is also a Director of Temenos which runs graduate and postgraduate courses in person-centred psychotherapy and counselling and supervision. He is the author of over fifty papers and of four books in the field of therapy and social policy: *Mental Health Promotion* (Routledge, 1996); *Group Counselling*, (Sage, 1999); editor of *Transactional Analysis Approaches to Brief Therapy* (Sage, 2002); and (with Tony Merry) *Dictionary of Person-Centred Psychology* (Whurr, 2002). In 1997 he edited a special issue of the journal *Person-Centred Practice* on 'The person-centred approach and the political sphere', and in 2002 (with Louise Embleton Tudor) has edited another issue on 'Psyche and soma'. He is the editor of a series of books *Advancing Theory in Therapy* (Brunner-Routledge).

Mark Widdowson is a UKCP-registered psychotherapist and counsellor based in Sheffield. He is a qualified counsellor and has also trained in Transactional Analysis psychotherapy as well as being a level two thought field therapy practitioner. His background is in shiatsu and oriental medicine and prior to becoming a therapist he was a community mental health worker. During this time he and his team won one of the national mental health awards for working with people with complex problems who are difficult to engage. Mark has written about Gay Affirmative approaches to Transactional Analysis and Brief TA psychotherapy. He has a particular interest in the integration of TA with object relations and self-psychology. His other interests are working with young people, looked after children and care leavers, disorders of the self and survivors of abuse. He undertakes long term work, but also enjoys working in brief contracts with a wide variety of client groups. He teaches and supervises counsellors.

Foreword

This book is a bold and much needed undertaking. It is timely, highly organized, extremely informative and practical, with many useful suggestions. Colin Lago and Barbara Smith have done the counselling profession a great favour by gathering diverse authors to educate and stimulate those of us who are therapists. They encourage us to dig deep into our own blinkered spots of discriminatory practices.

I am honoured in being asked to write this foreword. Honoured, because a book on anti-discriminatory counselling practice is a pioneering contribution, asking therapists to examine their own beliefs and cultural stereotypes as they face their clients. Colin Lago and I met as participants of an intensive person-centered weekend where we were all exploring our personal issues in relation to diversity. We discovered it is not always easy to face one's own racist, sexist, or discriminatory behaviour. However it is necessary and enlightening and brings us closer to the oneness of humanity.

I also feel humbled in being asked to write this piece because I am a white, upper-middle-class, heterosexual, elder American retired from my psychotherapy practice. There is a part of me that says a therapist who has experienced extreme discrimination should be writing this, perhaps a black, lesbian, disabled person. However, I have experienced my own second-class citizenship as a woman, which turned me into an active feminist aged forty. Also, my longing for social justice in a world full of discriminatory practices is deep. I believe, as the editors and authors of these chapters believe, that we must look into our personal attitudes and cultural history to become counsellors for those who have experienced discrimination. Although our intentions may be good, there is a great deal we need to learn from those who have led a life of oppression and discrimination. It is this openness to the experiences of others that I wish to address.

I proudly carry the philosophical legacy of my father, Carl Rogers, who was one of the founders of humanistic psychology and the author of *Client-centered Therapy and the Person-centered Approach*. It is his extensive research into the core conditions that foster the client's growth that is relevant here. The conditions of empathic listening, congruence and unconditional positive regard are key to the client–counsellor relationship. The client-centered approach emphasizes understanding the world as the client experiences it. As we create a safe, supportive, accepting climate and listen deeply to the experiences of our clients, they peel away their own layers of defence and self-doubt. By listening empathically to their rage and pain at experiences of exclusion, abuse, and discrimination and the deep scars these leave in their self-esteem, we allow them to go through the dark tunnel of despair into the light of self-care, self-esteem and personal empowerment.

Entering into the frame of reference of the client sounds easy. It is not. It means leaving aside our own need to be an authority figure or have the answers. It is also true that as we put aside our ego needs to under-stand the felt experience of the client, we open ourselves to our own per-sonal change; something not all therapists are eager to do. One way to learn about discrimination and oppression is to listen in depth, without judgement to our clients, friends and colleagues. This, along with educat-ing ourselves (as Graham Perlman suggests) through literature, art, films, friends, and examining our internalized cultural beliefs, will help us to become better counsellors.

It will also help us to review the ways in which we have felt personally discriminated against when we were clients. How well I remember the white male therapist who assumed I should stay in my role as supporter of my husband's work rather than step out into the professional world myself. In contrast, a person-centered, white, male therapist listened patiently to me as I explored my sense of having 'lost myself' in my marriage. At that time I no longer knew who I was, nor did I have any self-esteem. I was seriously considering ending my life. However, by being deeply heard (which is so healing in and of itself) and by being con-sidered a person of worth by my therapist as well as reading some early feminist literature, I realized that as a female I had a 'right to be me'. Now as a teacher of therapists and a group facilitator, I am keenly aware of women in that same predicament of living a life determined by the culture of the times. I am able to hear their anger and internalized self-deprecation and help them learn about the society that has insisted they hide their strength and power.

I bring forth my own example to point out that as therapists we can learn by sharing our experiences of discrimination when we were clients. Telling our personal stories of feeling misunderstood, or oppressed, or abused as a client will help us learn from each other, regardless of race, age, religion, gender or sexual orientation. Unlike many books that dis-cuss the particular symptoms and problems of the client, these authors put the emphasis where it belongs, on the beliefs, values, and practices of the counsellor.

The very insightful anti-racist counselling practice chapter by Oye Agoro had me stopping to re-read each page as she clearly defines the characteristics and behaviours of both black and white internalized racism. With each description of the White Identity Model I kept asking myself, 'Am I like this?' 'Do I do this?' Uncomfortable as it may be to say 'yes' at times, it is far better to acknowledge our prejudices and learn how to change our consciousness rather than continue perpetrating injustices. With each chapter in this book, there are excellent suggestions for identifying and working through our own discriminatory practices.

In the chapter on gay affirmative practice I was moved by the descriptions of those who are well-intentioned yet might give a smirk, or a glance or a subtle comment that tells the gay person they shouldn't exist. Perlman invites all practitioners to use the full range of their creativity and responsiveness to become caring, empathic counsellors for all human beings.

I was pleased to see the chapter by Barbara Smith and Mark Widdowson, on working with children, included in this book. It really gets to the heart of what we need to be doing to create a safer society for our children, to hear their voices, not just in the therapy room, but also in our schools and communities.

This pioneering book insists that the training of counsellors include their own self-analysis in the world of both subtle and not-so-subtle discriminatory practices. It challenges us to discover how we are racist, ageist, and sexist, homophobic or insensitive to those who are disabled or have religious beliefs other than our own. Yet, as a reader I never felt blamed, put-down or ignorant. Somehow these authors have written about very emotionally loaded subjects without putting the reader in a defensive stance. I found each chapter an invitation to open new doors to my mind and spirit. The final chapters give us concepts and training ideas to promote self-awareness and ways of making a difference to create a more just society.

Natalie Rogers PhD., author of: *Emerging Woman: A Decade of Midlife Transitions*, and *The Creative Connection: Expressive Art as Healing*.

Acknowledgements

This book came into being at a special moment in time involving two synchronous, co-incidental events. Firstly, the series editor Colin Feltham, had proposed and discussed such a book to me over a sandwich lunch. Upon my return to the office that day I was asked to telephone a 'Barbara Smith from Liverpool' who had rung while I was out. Barbara had called to say that she had enjoyed reading the book I had written with Joyce Thompson on Race, Culture and Counselling and that she thought another one needed doing on anti-discrimination and counselling. I explained that I had just that lunchtime been discussing such an idea and that we should talk further. My first and personal acknowledgement then is to both Colin Feltham who had the idea and to Barbara, the co-editor of this volume who also had the idea! We are indebted to all the chapter writers for their contributions and commitment to the overall mission of this book. Indeed, we have to thank them also for forbearance during a period when editing work on the book had to take a back seat as both of us were simultaneously caring for our very sick mothers who passed away last summer. This book therefore is also dedicated to them. An important thank you to my family – Gill, Becky and James – who continue to tolerate a pre-occupied dad and to all colleagues and friends who have inspired and supported me in the aspirations towards social justice embedded in this book.

Colin Lago

Thanks to Colin Lago who, without even having met me, trusted me to take on this project with him. It has been an honour to work with someone who believes so deeply in social justice. I would like to acknowledge the wonderful support of my friends and colleagues Alison, Brian, Helen, Jane, Karen and Mary. Barbara Webster for her kindness and nurturing. Kaye Richards has been an inspiration and her enthusiasm for the book has been tireless. Thanks to Andrea Cropper for teaching me over many years about the nature of oppression and its impact on our world. To Ronnie Murphy for his invaluable perspective on children's rights. To my students who so bravely and openly discuss these issues in ways which help us all to grow and to my clients who teach me so much about surviving oppression. A special thanks to my children Wendy and Gary for their love and patience. And to you, reader, for caring enough to pick up this book.

Barbara Smith

Every effort has been made to trace all the copyright holders, but if any have been inadvertently overlooked the publishers will be pleased to make the necessary arrangement at the first opportunity.

Figure 2.1: J. Katz, 'The Sociopolitical Nature of Counselling.' *Counselling Psychologist*, 13: 615–24, 1985. Copyright © 1985 by J. Katz. Reprinted by permission of Sage Publications Inc.

Figure 6.1: DfEE, *Promoting Children's Mental Health within Early Years and School Settings*, 2001. Reproduced with kind permission of HMSO.

1   *Ethical Practice and Best Practice*

Colin Lago and Barbara Smith

> Counselling and psychotherapy have often been criticized for focusing on the psychology of the individual and on the internal life of the client while ignoring the impact of the social, economic and cultural environment in which people live. (Feltham & Horton, 2000: 24)

Over recent years there has been a critically growing concern that the counselling and psychotherapy profession has been broadly dominated by middle class values and has been accessed mostly by those from privileged groups in society. People from marginalized groups (for example, people with physical or learning disabilities, black people, unwaged people etc.) are less likely to have had access to, been able to afford, or been referred to therapeutic services. Notwithstanding the above trends in the use of available services, the British Association for Counselling and Psychotherapy (BACP) has increasingly moved towards the adoption of counsellor accreditation and ethical criteria that are broadly socially inclusive and anti-discriminatory in intention, requiring members to have considered and sought training in this complex arena.

We come from the perspective that anti-oppressive/anti-discriminatory practice is both ethical practice and best practice (Thompson, 1993; Smith, 1999). We have used two different umbrella terms, 'anti-discriminatory' and 'anti-oppressive' practice. Burke & Dalrymple (1996) draw the general distinction between these two terms as that of acknowledging the legal underpinning of anti-discrimination, supported by a range of government acts, laws, policies and practices, and the humane concerns embodied in anti-oppressive practice. Thompson describes the link between discrimination (the unequal distribution of power, rights and resources) and oppression (the experience of hardship and injustice) – 'One of the main outcomes of discrimination is oppression' (1998, 78).

This book then, hails from a deeply held value base; that of seeking to explore and challenge oppressive and discriminatory practices in (and outside of) the field of therapy, and to advocate theories and modes of therapeutic and political interaction which respect the autonomy, capacities and the social position of the client.

That stated, we want to acknowledge the complexity and challenge that faces the professional field and the individual practitioner who takes up this often painful, confusing and isolating quest. Ironically, the challenge here is for the counsellor to change, rather than the client, and our invitation to readers is to dare to really feel the consequences of assuming this deeply philosophic stance in their personal and professional transactions with others. Taking on the ideas contained within this book will inevitably cause a shift in one's comfort zones, the journey being one of moving from a position of safety to the unknown, where there are many more questions than answers, more uncertainties than certainties, and possibly more critics than supporters.

In an absorbing article on the values of independent thinking and radicalism, Christopher Hitchens quotes his grandmother who had given him a bible in which she had written her favourite texts, one being 'Thou shalt not follow a multitude to do evil' (Hitchens, 2001). Independent thinking is a courageous stance needed for this journey. It is easy to become tired, demoralized and de-motivated, resorting to received modes of thinking and practice. A return to the comfortable old ways! Experience has taught us, however, that meeting these challenges brings rewards in terms of our relationships with other people, including our clients and students, and indeed with ourselves.

Historical learnings from a sister profession

The psychotherapeutic field is somewhat advantaged here in that the social work profession has for a long time been concerned with anti-discriminatory (ADP) and anti-oppressive (AOP) practice. We may therefore learn from these developments and indeed errors that have been tested, researched, taught and criticized whilst also recognizing the important differences between the two professions.

Thompson (1993) traces some of the historical roots underlying this rationale for social work. The 1960s were a significant period, he argues, in a number of ways. First, feminist thought made leaps forward, gaining recognition as a 'liberation movement'. Issues of equal rights and equality of opportunity became firmly established on the political agenda. Also, during the 1960s issues surrounding the oppression of 'ethnic minorities', and racial discrimination achieved more prominence politically, socially and in the mass media.

Thompson also notes the general popular tendency towards the raising of consciousness inspired by both the drug culture and political radicalism. The late '60s saw the emergence of the student protest movement, a time, he notes, 'of idealism and anti-establishment challenge of the status quo' (1993: 3).

Within the field of mental health and illness, writers such as Thomas Szasz (1970) & R.D. Laing (1965, 1967) radically challenged the contemporary views of the time, forever influencing subsequent thought and practice in this field of human distress.

Formerly dominated by a psychoanalytic view, social work came under the newer influence of sociology, with its emphasis on social processes and institutions rather than the previous, tighter, individualized focus upon the person. A series of legislative developments by government supported these general tendencies of the time, including the Race Relations Acts (1965, 1968, 1976), the Equal Pay Act (1970) and the Sex Discrimination Act (1975).

The broader field of therapeutic endeavour (counselling, psychotherapy, clinical psychology) has similarly and inevitably been influenced by the social trends, events, debates, academic discourses and government legislation in recent decades, though given its powerful underlying value base, geared towards the assistance of the individual (predominantly), the major focus of much training and professional practice has remained within the individualized, psychologized perspectives of personal change and transformation. Despite this, there has been a wide range of published voices within the field urging therapists to become familiar with the differing arenas of discrimination and oppression in society, drawing therapists' attention to the socially, culturally and politically structured nature of human beings' existence (see D'Ardenne & Mahtani (1989), Eleftheriadou (1994), Lago & Thompson (1989, 1996, 1997), and Pedersen et al. (1981) on matters of race and culture; Chaplin (1989) on counselling and gender; Corker (1994), Makin (1995) and Segal (1997) on disability issues; Davies & Neal (1996) on gay and lesbian issues; Carolin (1995) on working with children; Craig (1998) on attitudes to ageing; Kearney (1996) and Bromley (1994) on class and Thorne (1998) on spirituality).

Each of these social arenas has distinct characteristics and multiple discourses, in addition to their similarities and interconnections. This will become clearer as the following chapters are examined. Any simple attempt, therefore, to assemble these various facets into an apparently over-arching homogenous system of AOP and ADP in therapy will be doomed from the start (Wilson & Beresford, 2000). It seems to us that, for many therapists, the issues that they develop a 'passion' for and sensitivity to often reflect their own previous histories and experiences. It is helpful to broaden this out, however, to develop this knowledge base and sensitivity to the many areas of social life in which oppression occurs. This is a major challenge, particularly as this knowledge itself is specifically determined by the biases of background, training, readings and experiences, both personal and professional.

The client and the therapist in the context of 'society'

> Civilization as we know it is based on the violation and domination of subordinates by elites. Violation, domination and hegemony are common to all oppression. All oppression is heinous, dehumanizing and confusing. (Burstow, 1992)

A central tenet of this book is that the individual and the society within which they are raised are inextricably intertwined. The power of the 'social context' to shape a person's sense of identity, esteem, values, beliefs, behaviours and perceptions is enormous and some would argue total, as in the South African proverb, 'I am because we are'. How and where we are raised, what stories and experiences we are exposed to – all are ingredients of the interconnectedness between the growing child, the immediate carers (most frequently the family) and key agents of socialization such as education, religion, health, politics, law and communicated messages embodied in the media. All have an (often unconscious) influence on our views of ourselves, of others and the world. At the Institute for the Healing of Racism, there is a view (and one to which we subscribe) that discrimination and oppression damage *everyone*. We damage our boy children by teaching them that they are superior to girl children; we damage our white children by teaching them, however unintentionally and subtly, that they are superior to black children. The confusion and pathology which follows really belongs to the *oppressor,* but is projected onto others. Nelson Mandela suggests 'The oppressed and the oppressor alike are robbed of their humanity'. The healing of this begins with awareness.

Given the above, we recommend an examination of the impact of *ideology, hegemony* and *discourse,* and a context of how they operate within society and upon individuals.

Ideology

Thompson defines ideology as 'a set of ideas which are associated with a particular set of social arrangements' (1993: 24). A review of the concept will reveal that, despite its relative youth as a concept, the analysis and definitions of ideology itself are a cauldron of competing ideas and hypotheses (McLellan, 1995: 2).

Continuing his appraisal of the term, Thompson says: 'the ideas base safeguards the power base. In fact this is what characterises ideology: the power of ideas, operating in the interest of power relations' (1993: 24). Hall notes 'ideology helps to sustain social order because it is part and parcel of the power relations in society – it influences how power works and how conflict is expressed and managed' (1986: 6).

Both Althusser (1971) and Berger (1996) have noted the process of internalization, of the taking in, by people, of the dominant ideologies so that these ideologies become internalized and believed and the relationship between that which has been internalized and the external source(s) from which it emanated may often remain unknown and concealed. We are all therefore subject to the influences of many ideologies to the extent we fully believe they represent our own view of things. To dig beneath the surface of these simplified belief structures is so important, yet so difficult to the discerning therapeutic practitioner.

Hegemony

Hegemony, the second mechanism to be considered, is described as 'political dominance of one power over others in a group in which all are supposedly equal' (Hutchinson, 1993). An example of this would be where one group or social collectivity gained power, status, and position at the expense of other less favoured groups.

Hegemony is therefore closely linked to the notion of exploitation, although not necessarily in any deliberate or intentional sense. It is also closely linked to the notion of ideology for it is often through the vehicle of ideology that hegemony operates (Thompson, 1993). Part of the ideological base of hegemony is the idea of an 'out group', a group of people defined in negative terms and assigned an inferior status. This tendency is quite clearly, therefore, part of the process of discrimination and oppression.

Hegemony is especially important in societies in which electoral politics and public opinion are significant factors, and in which social practice is seen to depend on consent to certain dominant ideas that in fact express the needs of a dominant class (Williams, 1983).

Discourse

The Concise Oxford Dictionary (1974) describes discourse as a talk, conversation, dissertation, treatise or sermon – 'to hold forth in speech or writing on a subject', or 'a serious conversation between people on a particular subject' (Collins, 1991).

Discourse analysis has become a significant research area across the social sciences, in recognition of the fact that any interaction between two people is shaped and informed by the processes they both bring to it, these processes being both internal (to each) and external (the other) and relational (between them).

In attempting to draw together the implications of these three dynamic social processes we may observe the very profound, complex interweaving of thought, beliefs, values, influences and perspectives that perpetually surround and engage us in everyday life. In short, we, as editors of this text also have to acknowledge our part in contributing to the shaping of an alternative hegemony within counselling and psychotherapy through the very writing and editing of this book.

The above dominant and dominating socio-cultural-political processes may be identified as significant contributors to oppressive and discriminatory beliefs and practices in society.

Identity development and the 'Other'

Important research has been conducted (and much critiqued) in the last two decades on the consequences of such processes upon people's sense of identity, particularly in relation to those who are seen to be 'different'. Much of this research has been conducted within the field of racial and ethnic identity formation and, we believe, has much to inform those in the counselling/psychotherapy profession.

Carter quotes a personal communication from A.J. Franklin who notes that 'when writing about race one constantly struggles with the question of how much emphasis to give historical, socio-economic, socio-political, intrapsychic and contemporary events' (1995: 2). As authors, we are sensitive to Franklin's notion of the difficulties in knowing where to place the emphasis, though through the above descriptions of ideology, hegemony and discourse we more specifically wish to acknowledge the 'Gordian knot' of complexity that nevertheless systematically communicates different messages of worth, value and treatment to different people and groups within society.

Carter (1995) argues that race has been and continues to be the ultimate measure of social exclusion and inclusion (Carter is writing here of the American context, though there are some similarities in the UK) because it is a visible factor that historically and currently determines the rules and bounds of social and cultural interaction (Kovel, 1984; Smedley, 1993).

The following chapters refer to the experiences of people from a range of different groups within society, some of whom are visible and thus identifiable in some sense as 'other' than the dominant group. For the purpose of a clear example however, let us return to the identity formation models referred to above which are also psychological models (specifically pertaining to the USA where this work was developed) and which offer within-racial group variations as well. In Carter's view race and racial identity are integral aspects of personality and human development (1995: 4). Yet, paradoxically, the personal meaning and significance of 'race' has not been extended to white Americans (11).

Taking this perspective as the stimulus, it seems that the categorization of 'otherness' is attributed to those not conforming or belonging to a dominant 'norm.' From Carter's quote above that notes white as a 'norm' we may also recognize other hegemonic/ideological positions relative to those occupying the position of the 'other' – those in the dominant group have little awareness of their position as being white, or able bodied, or heterosexual, etc. 'Norm' therefore, somehow, remains unquestionable, not worthy of exploration, indeed out of awareness. Rochlin (1992: 203–4) wryly challenges this in his 'Heterosexual Questionnaire' – asking heterosexuals to consider such questions as 'What do you think caused your heterosexuality?', 'Is it possible that your heterosexuality is just a phase you may grow out of?' and 'To whom have you disclosed your heterosexuality? How did they react?' Similar questions are all too common to gay men and lesbians.

The lived complexity of all these societal and social dynamics provides a somewhat clouded, dense, confused and contradictory picture, yet multiple waves of research continue to point to socially and professionally embedded interactions and behaviours that result in discrimination and oppression of those from marginalized groups. The various forms of oppression mediated through the dominant ideologies, hegemonies and discourses (which support discriminatory behaviours) impact greatly upon the identities of people from these marginalized groups, at the very least in terms of:

- Alienation, isolation and marginality;
- Economic position and life chances;
- Confidence and self esteem; and
- Social expectations, career opportunities etc. (Thompson, 1993: 151)

There are no simple, overarching assumptions that can be made in terms of the forms that oppression and discrimination take. Different groups experience complex patterns of oppression and indeed (within the groupings considered in this text) individuals may experience multiple oppressions (see Chapter 10 for further discussion).

The power of language

> Sticks and stones may break my bones but words can never hurt me.
>
> (A children's saying)

Language, often the very tool through which we conduct our therapeutic processes, is a complex and ever changing 'minefield'. Any conversation with others, let alone that conducted between counsellor and client in the therapeutic situation, alerts us to the power of language to buoy us up or pull us down, to enhance self-esteem or to sabotage self-confidence, to inflict pain or to encourage, to influence positively or negatively, to manipulate or to understand (Lago, 1997). In this regard we are most concerned about the sensitivity of the therapist's use of language (and para-verbal behaviour) in relation to their clients.

'Words really are important', argues Will Hutton in an article critical of the political influences of the American Right that has sneered at ideas and ideals of political correctness (2001). In drawing attention to the politicized usage of words, Hutton demonstrates powerfully how (in this case) the American Right was quick to declare war on the cultural manifestations of liberalism by levelling the charge of political correctness against its exponents and in so doing, discredit the whole political project. Setting out with the intention of sensitizing each other to the power and impact of language, 'political correctness' eventually became a term of some derision that subsequently evoked very strong reactions in people concerned not to be 'policed' in their use of language, however apparent the justice of the cause. One of the difficulties here is a tendency for people to take an oversimplified view of the issue of language use. For example, one of the authors has often been asked by students to tell them what they are 'allowed' to say and what they are 'not allowed' to say, fearful of being attacked or shamed for saying the 'wrong' things. We cannot ignore the power of language in maintaining oppressive power relations. Thompson (1998) explains that the question of language use is not 'a simple lexicon of taboo words that are to be avoided' but is a complex and powerful vehicle, which contributes to the maintenance of oppression. He highlights the importance of power dynamics in interactions between workers and service users in the caring professions, identifying a number of key issues:

- Jargon – the use of specialized language, creating barriers, which reinforce power differences
- Stereotypes – terms used to refer to people from different groups i.e. older people as 'old dears'
- Stigma – terms such as mental handicap carry a damaging stigma
- Exclusion – this might be inadvertently asking a Muslim what his Christian name is, rather than his first name
- Depersonalization – this relates to terms such as 'the elderly', rather than 'older people' and 'the mentally ill', rather than 'people with mental distress'

A common argument in discussions about the power of language is that language not only describes reality, it *determines* reality. Thompson quotes Spender:

> Through my language and socialization I did learn to see as *sensible* many arrangements in my society which an 'outsider' (who did not share my socialization) would find absurd. So at one stage I did learn, for example, that it was sensible to give the least educational experience to those who appeared to take longer to learn. I did learn that it was sensible to classify some forms of skin pigmentation as possessing mystical powers. I did learn that it was sensible that one half of the population should be paid for their work while the other half should not. I did learn that it was sensible to ensure the survival of the species by amassing a vast arsenal that could destroy the planet many times over. And I did learn that it was sensible to see men as superior. (1990: 3)

We believe it is critically important to explore our use of language as therapists. Mindful of some of the settings in which counsellors work and the specific difficulties clients struggle with, we need to be sensitive to some of the words in common use and which are in effect, deeply offensive. Working with people who have dependency problems, for example; do we subscribe to terms like 'drug user', 'drug abuser', 'drug pusher' or 'recreational drug use'? Do we use terms like 'alcoholic' 'alcohol abuser/misuser'? It is only in recent years that we have developed a language to describe the phenomenon of child sexual abuse. Previously there was no discourse and children's distress went (as it often still does) unheeded. Burstow (1992: 202) refers to 'eating disorders' as 'troubled eating'. She says 'There is nothing more orderly than the precise regimen that women who are anorexic follow'. We hear of 'date rape' and somehow it is thought to be less traumatic or damaging than other rape, and which term most appropriately describes the reality of women who are intimidated, tortured, battered and sometimes murdered by their partners – 'domestic violence' or 'woman battering'? Burstow (1992) refers to 'psychiatric survivors', having been 'psychiatrized' by the system and Wilson & Beresford (2000) use the term 'people with madness and distress' rather than the more sanitized 'mental health service users'. These are just some of the questions we invite readers to consider when contemplating their use of language with clients.

Though perhaps only as an adjunct to this specific aspect of the chapter, Lee (2000) draws our attention to the developing field of 'cyber counselling'. Given the reliance of cyber communication, at present, on being word based, the cyber counsellor will have to pay detailed attention to their use of language with cyber clients to avoid discrimination and disempowerment. In short, the therapist will need, even more, to become a 'wordsmith' (Lago, 1996).

A critique of the critique

The fields of knowledge, research and practice in relation to social justice and social inclusion are ever changing in approach, language and emphasis. Each shift of position, philosophy or policy may cause great anxiety, concern and disagreement. This is inevitable within the process of cultural and societal change, but at the personal level, individual practitioners may be sorely challenged to grapple with new and emerging ideas, particularly when they may have strongly held, earlier personal positions on these subjects.

An earlier section of this chapter took the example set by the sister profession of social work as a template for understanding the essential thrust of this book, that of aspiring to practices and policies in counselling which are anti-oppressive and anti-discriminatory. It is to the same profession, or indeed a critique of it, we now return in the hope that, as a body of practice, we may not repeat what Wilson and Beresford argue has happened to social work. They say of their critique:

> Whilst acknowledging the emancipatory aspirations of anti-oppressive practice, it also considers its regressive potential. … This discussion highlights the failure, so far, to significantly involve service users and their organizations in the development of anti-oppressive theory and practice. It considers how the ideology and structures of anti-oppressive social work impact upon service users; the problems raised by expert appropriation of users knowledge and experiences … (2000: 553)

A major concern they express is that of the silence of clients' voices (and clients' organizations) in a consultation process that takes their opinions and experiences into account in informing new practice and practitioners. The therapeutic profession does have the advantage that trainee counsellors experience their own therapy and are therefore, at least for a time, 'service users' – a somewhat different situation to that of most social workers. Readers will gather from the biographies of the authors of this book that most have experience of surviving some form(s) of discrimination or oppression either through being a woman, a gay man, a lesbian, being black, working class, disabled or older. We each come from a place of commitment to and passion for promoting good ethical practice, which acknowledges the social and political nature of counselling and of clients' concerns.

We invite the reader to develop awareness of the social and political 'backdrop' to their clients' stories. Does this woman, for example stay in a violent relationship because of her personal psychology, or do issues of poverty and powerlessness, and lack of appropriate support services contribute to her problems? Is she a black woman? What would her (and her children's) experience be, of a refuge where all the other women, including workers, were white? And if she were a lesbian; how might she be received or understood by her heterosexual peers?

Is this older gay man isolated and lonely because he is shy and lacking in confidence or is there a deep fear of homophobic abuse due to previous experiences; or is it because gay scenes are often exclusive, seemingly valuing only youth and 'beauty'? Is this black child's school refusal 'separation anxiety' or is it due to a fear of daily racist bullying, in a school that has no bullying policy and where the staff deny the existence of racism?

Wilson and Beresford pose very challenging questions to anti-oppressive social work practice from their perspective as both lecturers in and users of social work. In short they are led, from this standpoint, to pose the fundamental question, is the very concept or possibility of anti-oppressive social work theory or practice, at least as it is currently produced and practised, possible? Just what is it, they ask, that constitutes anti-oppressive social work? A complex contradiction is presented here, as anti-oppressive practice is generally offered as an unquestionable good. Yet there is little recognition of the possibility that such ideas or theories could, in themselves, be oppressive or reproduce social injustice.

As counsellors we might ask ourselves similar questions.

Summary

Within these chapters, we offer an opportunity to reflect (as counsellors and citizens), on our attitudes and received ideas about different social 'groupings' and their experiences of counselling and wider society. We have been cautious about not wanting to produce a 'how to' text, for instance, lists of characteristics about communities and cultures, focusing on the client, rather than our own need to be independent in our thinking and abandon ideas and practices which perpetuate discrimination and oppression. We invite readers to consider the concepts of *anti*-discrimination and *anti*-oppression in that these require a *proactive* approach. As therapists, our subtle and unintentional processes can support the broad social pattern of discrimination, and anti-oppressive practice (as distinct from non-oppressive) requires us to question our own practice and challenge individuals and institutions (in particular our own profession, however well intentioned), which maintain the oppression of our clients.

The only real 'how to' we offer is that of beginning to see that the pathology, and the need for healing and change, in this context, lies within the oppressor, *us,* and the oppressive structures which *create* and *exacerbate* our clients' distress.

Key points:

We have found the following key issues helpful in developing our practice with all clients.

- As therapists we are often agents of change and can promote change on a political as well as an individual level
- Acknowledge that racism and other oppressions are part of British society and as such we must recognize these in ourselves
- Address our own denial and avoidance of these issues through effective supervision
- Commit ourselves to ongoing reflective practice: the political climate is fluid and changing
- Challenge oppression in all its forms, even when it feels uncomfortable
- Examine the use of terms that may be degrading or hurtful
- Affirm our client's cultural identity, acknowledging their survival skills and coping mechanisms
- Be sensitive to issues of isolation, due to marginalization, and clients' need for outside support
- Offer alternative views about distorted beliefs about self where the client has been misinformed about their own and other social groups
- Be aware that black, gay, female or disabled clients etc. may not be bringing issues of race, gender, sexuality or disability to therapy
- Recommend reading (bibliotherapy) and films which address the issues the client may bring
- Use consultation or referral if we feel inadequately equipped to help our clients

- Take steps to become more knowledgeable about other cultures, life-styles, values and histories
- Broaden our range of helping styles to accommodate different cultural expectations and needs
- Undertake to find out what community groups and resources are available for clients who want to contact people with a shared experience of oppression
- Align ourselves with struggles against oppression outside the therapy room
- Examine policy which might unintentionally exclude people
- Make anti-oppressive practice integral to training courses rather than just add-on modules
- Start now

References

Althusser, L. (1971) 'Ideology and Ideological State Apparatuses', in *Lenin and Philosophy*. London: New Left Books.

Anthony, K. (2001) 'Online Relationships & Cyber Infidelity'. *Counselling & Psychotherapy Journal*. British Association for Counselling and Psychotherapy (BACP). Vol. 12, No. 9, pp. 38–9.

Berger, P.L. (1996) *Invitation to Sociology*. Harmondsworth: Penguin.

Bimrose, J. (1993) 'Counselling and Social Context', in R. Bayne and P. Nicholson (eds), *Counselling & Psychotherapy for Health Professionals*. London: Chapman & Hall.

Bromley, E. (1994) 'Social Class & Psychotherapy Revisited'. Paper presented at the Annual Conference of the British Psychological Society, Brighton.

Burke, B. & Dalrymple, J. (1996) *Anti-Oppressive Practice – Social Care and the Law*. Buckingham: Open University Press.

Burstow, B. (1992) *Radical Feminist Therapy – Working in the Context of Violence*. Thousand Oaks, CA: Sage.

Carolin, B. (1995) 'Working with Children in a Family and Divorce Centre'. *Counselling: Journal of British Association for Counselling* (BAC). Vol. 6, No. 3, pp. 207–10.

Carter, R.T. (1995) *The Influence of Race and Racial Identity in Psychotherapy: Towards a Racially Inclusive Model*. New York: John Wiley and Sons.

Chaplin, J. (1989) 'Counselling & Gender', in S. Palmer & G. McMahon (eds) *Handbook of Counselling*. London: Routledge and Rugby: BAC.

Christopher, E. (2001) 'Black Hands in a Black Trade'. *Times Higher Educational Supplement*. 29 June, p. iv.

Collins School Dictionary (1991) London: Harper Collins.

The Concise Oxford Dictionary (1974) Oxford: Oxford University Press.

Corker, M. (1994) *Counselling – The Deaf Challenge*. London: Jessica Kingsley Publishing.

Craig, Y. (1998) 'Attitudes to Ageing: Its Social Constitution, Deconstruction and Reconstitution'. *Counselling*. BAC, Vol. 9, No. 1, pp. 49–53.

D'Ardenne, P. & Mahtani, A. (1989) *Transcultural Counselling in Action*. London: Sage.

Davies, N. & Neal, C. (1996) *Pink Therapy*. Buckingham: Open University Press.

Eleftheriadou, Z. (1994) *Transcultural Counselling*. London: Central Books.

Feltham, C. & Horton, I. (eds) (2000) *Handbook of Counselling & Psychotherapy*. London: Sage.

Gammack, G. (2001) 'Behind the Fireplace'. *Counselling and Psychotherapy Journal*. BACP Vol. 12., No. 9, pp. 14–19.

Hall, S. (1986) Managing Conflict, Producing Consent. Open University Unit 21 of D102, Social Science: A Foundation Course.

Helms, J.E. (1984) 'Towards a Theoretical Model of the Effects of Race on Counselling: A Black & White Model'. *The Counselling Psychologist*. Vol. 12, pp. 153–65.

Hitchens, C. (2001) 'Letters to a Young Contrarian'. *The Guardian, Saturday Review*. 10 November, p. 3.

Hutchinson Encyclopaedia (1993) *The 1994 Edition*. Norwich: Helicon Publishing.

Hutton, W. (2001) 'Words Really Are Important, Mr. Blunkett'. *The Observer*. 16 December, p. 26.

Kearney, A. (1996) *Counselling, Class and Politics*. Manchester: PCCS Books.

Kovel, J. (1984) *White Racism*. New York: Columbia University Press.

Lago, C.O. & Thompson, J. (1989) 'Counselling & Race', in W. Dryden et al. *Handbook of Counselling in Britain*. London: Tavistock-Routledge. (Also in S. Palmer (ed.) (2002) *Multicultural Counselling: A Reader*. London: Sage).

Lago, C.O. in collaboration with Thompson, J. (1996) *Race, Culture & Counselling*. Buckingham: Open University Press.

Lago, C.O. (1996) 'Computer Therapeutics: A New Challenge for Counsellors & Psychotherapists'. *Counselling*: Journal of the BAC. Vol. 17, No. 4, pp. 287–9.

Lago, C.O. (1997) 'Race, Culture & Language: A Redefinition of Terms'. *RACE Journal*. BAC. No. 12, Spring.

Lago, C.O. & Thompson, J. (1997) 'The Triangle With Curved Sides: Sensitivity to Issues of Race and Culture in Supervision' in G. Shipton (ed.) *Supervision of Psychotherapy & Counselling*. Buckingham: Open University Press.

Laing, R.D. (1965) *The Divided Self*. Harmondsworth: Penguin.

Laing, R.D. (1967) *The Politics of Experience and the Bird of Paradise*. Harmondsworth: Penguin.

Lee, C.C. (2000) 'Cybercounselling and Empowerment: Bridging the Cultural Divide', in J.W. Bloom & G.R. Walz (eds), *Cybercounseling and Cyberlearning: Strategies for the Millennium*. American Counseling Association: Alexandria.

Makin, T. (1995) 'The Social Model of Disability'. *Counselling*. BAC. Vol. 6, No. 4, p. 275.

McLellan, D. (1995) *Ideology–Second Edition*. Buckingham: Open University Press.

Observer Special Report. (2001) Race in Britain. *The Observer*. 25 November.

Pedersen, P., Draguns, J.G., Lonner, W.J. & Trimble, J.E. (1981) *Counselling Across Cultures*. Hawaii: East–West Center.

Potter, J. & Wetherall, M. (1987) *Discourse & Social Psychology*. London: Sage.

Rochlin, M. (1992) 'Heterosexual Questionnaire', in W.J. Blumenfeld (ed.), *Homophobia: How We All Pay The Price*. Boston, MA: Beacon Press.

Rowe, D. (2001) 'The Story of Depression'. *Counselling and Psychotherapy Journal*. BACP. Vol. 12, No. 9, pp. 4–5.

Scott, N. (2001) 'A Place of Safety? How Can Women Feel Safe in the Company of Men if they have Felt Threatened at a Previous Stage in their Lives?' *Your Voice in Sheffield Mental Health*. September/October. No. 18. Sheffield: SYAC Centre (Sheffield 538 JD).

Segal, J. (1997) 'Counselling People with Disabilities/Chronic Illnesses', in S. Palmer and G. McMahon (eds), *Handbook of Counselling* (second edition) London: Routledge.

Smedley, A. (1993) *Race in North America: Origin and Evolution of a World View*. Boulder, CO: Westview Press.

Smith, B. (1999) 'Potency, Permission, Protection & Politics'. *ITA News*. No. 55, Autumn, pp. 17–20.

Spender, D (1990) *Man Made Language*. London: Pandora.

Szasz, T. (1970) *The Manufacture of Madness: A Comparative Study of the Inquisition and the Mental Health Movement*. New York: Harper and Row.

Thompson, N. (1993) *Anti-Discriminatory Practice*. London: Macmillan.

Thompson, N. (1998) Promoting Equality – Challenging Discrimination and Oppression in the Human Services. London: Macmillan.

Thorne, B.J. (1998) *Person Centred Counselling & Christian Spirituality*. London: Whurr Publishers.

Williams, R. (1983) *Keywords – A Vocabulary of Culture & Society*. London: Flamingo.

Wilson, A. & Beresford, P. (2000) 'Anti-Oppressive Practice: Emancipation & Appropriation.' *British Journal of Social Work*. Vol. 30, p. 553–73.

2 Anti-racist Counselling Practice

Oye Agoro

There is a slow and growing awareness that as counsellors we have a professional responsibility to work competently with black[1] clients. Since October 2000 counsellors seeking accreditation through the British Association for Counselling and Psychotherapy now have to demonstrate their ability to work with issues of race and culture.

Among other events, the murder of Stephen Lawrence, a black teenager, by a gang of white youths in London in 1993, followed by a bungled police investigation and failure of the criminal justice system to convict anyone for the murder, has generated considerable discussion about racism[2] and the experiences of black people living in Britain.

Within counselling and psychotherapy, concerns have been raised about the provision of counselling for black clients centring on a number of issues. Research shows that many black clients have difficulty accessing counselling services for various reasons, ranging from the high cost of private counselling to GPs being reluctant to refer black clients (Kareem & Littlewood, 1992). Counsellors have been criticized for their inability to acknowledge the importance of social factors such as racism, sexism and class in their understanding of clients' experiences (Moodley & Perkins, 1990). Issues related to racism, and cultural and religious sensitivity, are not as yet integral parts of counsellor training.

Anti-racist counselling practice addresses issues of racism and cultural diversity within the therapeutic relationship and wider society. Anti-racist approaches are identifiable by their understanding of the way racism impacts on black and white people and their commitment to eliminating it.

Racism

Dominelli states that 'British racism is about the construction of social relations on the basis of an assumed inferiority of non-Anglo Saxon ethnic minority groups and flowing from this their exploitation and oppression. Racism is apparent in the minutiae of everyday life as well as in institutions and legislation that permeates every aspect of our personal and professional lives whether we are black or white' (1998: 6).

The Macpherson Report (1999), commissioned by the UK government as a result of the events surrounding the murder of Stephen Lawrence is the first government paper that acknowledges the existence of institutional racism. Macpherson suggested that 'Institutional racism is the collective failure of an organization to provide an appropriate professional service to people because of their colour, culture or ethnic origin. It can be seen or detected in processes, attitudes and behaviour, which amounts to discrimination through unwitting prejudice, ignorance, thoughtlessness, and racist stereotypes' (1999: 28).

In Britain, racism evolved from Britain's imperialistic history that has included the emergence of capitalism from the trans-Atlantic slave trade and the colonization of North America, along with the economic plunder and exploitation of peoples from Australasia, Africa, Asia and the Americas.

The myth of the superiority of the white race and the inferiority of non-white peoples has been the justification of this history. White scholars have rationalized white supremacy theories through pseudo-scientific/ biological explanations, arguing that black people have smaller brains or are at a lower level of evolution – primitive. They have put forward quasi-religious explanations, which have labelled black people as heathens, uncivilized, without souls, and being closer to nature, while white people or white men in particular embody culture. Perhaps most obviously there has been the phenomenon of associating people's skin colour to symbolic representations of white and black. White is portrayed as signifying spirituality, purity, goodness, divinity, and beauty and generally associated with positive characteristics, while black has been associated with evil, sin, dirtiness, death and mourning, sexual provocation, immorality, and a whole host of other negative connotations.

Racism exists in all the major institutions, including health, education, employment, law and housing, and impacts on the lives of black people in concrete ways that are observable and identifiable:

- The British Crime Survey estimated that in 1996, 382,000 crimes were motivated by racism.

- Black men and women born in the Caribbean and living in Britain are between 76 per cent – 110 per cent at greater risk of dying from strokes.
- In 1995/96 the unemployment rate for ethnic minorities was more than double the rate for the white population.
- In Greater London ethnic minorities form 45 per cent of the statutory homeless.
- In June 1997, the prison incarceration rate per 100,00 population in England and Wales was 1,249 for black people, 176 for white and 150 for Asians.
- Studies of the psychiatric system over the last 20 years show that black people are 50 per cent more likely than white people to be diagnosed as suffering from schizophrenia, detained in locked wards and given higher dosages of medication.

As well as the external reality, racism also affects black people's sense of self and the internal world in terms of thoughts, feelings and emotions. For some black people, their experiences of racism can be a significant or contributory factor in their decision to seek therapeutic help.

From a psychotherapeutic point of view it is important to recognize that racism is a product of the white psyche. In psychoanalytic terms, racism can clearly be viewed as a primitive defence mechanism, on a societal level where aspects of the individual and collective unconscious are split off and projected on to others. Undoubtedly there can be many interpretations of what underlies white racism. I believe that in part, it can be explained as a manifestation of the infantile and frail nature of the white racist psyche, and its consequent denial or inability to accept and acknowledge the shame and guilt of an ancestral and contemporary history of domination and exploitation of non-white peoples.

Internalized racism

No analysis of racism can be complete without an understanding of internalized racism. Internalized oppression is a key therapeutic concept that has relevance when working with anybody who experiences structural inequalities and oppression. Internalized racism becomes apparent when black people take on board and believe subconsciously and/or consciously the beliefs of white supremacy and the numerous black stereotypes that come from this.

The 'acting out' of white stereotypes of blackness, and other patterns of internalized racism are a reflection of the way black people survive the day-to-day realities of racism. For many black people, this acting out of white stereotypes of blackness has ensured their literal survival. A consequence of this survival strategy, however, is that it actively promotes white supremacy. Internalized racism dramatically affects the way that black people relate to each other and to white people. Expressions of internalized racism within the black communities are diverse, but include:

Acting out of white stereotypes of blackness

- Black stud/black whore: relates to the sexualization of black people, typically being portrayed as sexually uninhibited, provocative and predatory.
- Happy Go Lucky Clown – Uncle Sam: embodied in aspects of British culture such as *The Black and White Minstrel Show*. This stereotype relates to the white racist fantasy of having black people that are accepting of and happy with white supremacy.
- Criminal Yardie – West African Fraudster: relates to the criminalization of black people. The internalization and glorification of this stereotype can be seen in some aspects of black youth culture.
- Black Mama – Superwoman: embodied in the myth that romanticizes black women as the archetypal mother, and the associated expectation that black women should be nurturing of all people.

Acting out of colonial and plantation-like dynamics within black families and personal relationships

The legacy of colonization and slavery at times has its expression in patterns of behaviour within black families and relationships. These dynamics can take many forms and often include sexual, physical and verbal violence, repression of individuality and creativity, and an uncritical acceptance of hierarchical and authoritarian power structures.

Expressions of self-hatred

This includes black on black violence, evident in black gang warfare, skin bleaching, believing that white people are superior, and having a hatred of 'unrelaxed' hair. Expressions of self-hatred may be enacted within the counselling relationship. Some black clients can present with a conscious or unconscious belief that white people are superior, which can be expressed in a categorical insistence on seeing a white counsellor.

Acceptance and acting out of white skin colour hierarchies

In some black communities there is an admiring and coveting of light skin tones and a revulsion and hatred of dark skin. Some of the black clients I have seen have described how they or their siblings have been treated differently because of the colour of their skin, referred to as shadism. Within shadism there is often the attribution of personal characteristics to skin colour. As a counsellor I have seen shadism manifested in many ways. For example 'Rita', an Asian Caribbean woman with a diagnosis of paranoid schizophrenia, when distressed, heard voices telling her that she was a 'black bitch' and that her skin was 'rotting and smelling'. Rita grew up in the Caribbean, the darkest-skinned daughter in a family of six children. In Rita's family, negative personal characteristics were systematically attributed to darker skin colour. She was routinely told that she was sexually provocative, immoral, unclean and stupid, because she looked less Asian/European than her siblings. Rita's psychiatrist clearly saw her as having a medical condition, schizophrenia, and that she should be treated with medication. Although I do not doubt that psychotropic medication helped her cope with the voices (despite the unpleasant side effects), the approach that I chose to take was to focus on her identity as a black woman through a range of interventions aimed at encouraging an exploration of her identity as an Asian Caribbean woman, and her feelings about her mixed cultural heritage. I also provided more political interpretation of the voices, which involved talking about them as related to racism and connecting the voices to views held within her family and the Caribbean about race and culture. We also explored her family's experiences of racism and responses to it. This approach enabled Rita to view her voices as more than a symptom of a medical disease but as connected to her history and life experiences, which included sexual and racial violence in her childhood and present life.

Identity

As a counsellor it is important to have an understanding of white and black identity formation in order to work competently with racial and cultural issues. Our perceptions as counsellors about our own identities can have enormous implications for how we relate to clients, and the possible permutations for the therapeutic process. The Ethnic Identity Development models developed in America (Helms, 1984; Sue, 1998; Wren, 1962) are useful tools for identifying racial issues in counselling. They can also facilitate personal development and self-awareness for all counsellors.

In conceptualizing white identity formation under white supremacy, I have adapted Sue and Sue's (1998, 1999) White Identity Model (3).

White identity model

Conformity

At this level of awareness counsellors and clients are unlikely to see themselves in a racial and cultural way, but hold a belief that white British culture is superior and that other cultures are inferior. Typically, there is little awareness of their own beliefs and an assumption that their values are normal and universal. A common philosophy is that people are people and that differences are not important, known as 'colour blindness'. Counsellors generally deny black clients' experiences of pervasive racism and are likely to act out racial dynamics based on values of white supremacy. Clients are likely to hold a preference for white counsellors.

Dissonance – Conflict

There is an increasing realization of one's own cultural bias and recognition that white cultural values play an important part in oppressing minorities. Rationalization is often used to exonerate personal inactivity in combating racism and discrimination. Counsellors and clients are likely to experience conflict between appreciation for white British culture and an awareness of discrimination. White counsellors may have difficulty in responding consistently to black clients' experiences of discrimination and may be vulnerable to using the therapeutic process with clients to work through feelings about their own white identity.

Resistance & Immersion – 'White Liberal'

There is a questioning of one's own racism and an increasing awareness of how racism operates and its pervasiveness in white British culture, along with a growing social and political consciousness, and an acknowledgment of past personal collusion with racism. There is likely to be a tendency towards racial and cultural self-hatred and feeling ashamed of whiteness. Counsellors at this stage are prone to over identify with black clients and be pre-occupied with issues relating to race and culture at the expense of everything else. The counselling relationship is likely to be paternalistic; counsellors may experience difficulties in setting appropriate therapeutic boundaries as a result of anxiety about their own identity.

Introspection

There is a re-thinking of what it means to be white and an acknowledgment of past participation in racism and the benefits gained from white privilege. Counsellors will have awareness that racism is an integral part of British society along with an acceptance of whiteness and a desire to combat oppression. Counsellors at this stage are able to create a therapeutic environment where black clients' experiences of racism are heard and acknowledged. They are also likely to have a high level of self-awareness about their own cultural and racial identity but experience a high level of anxiety and loss, 'existential anxiety'.

Integrative Awareness – Freedom

Counsellors and clients have an understanding of self as a cultural and racial being, along with an awareness of the political and social nature of racism. Counsellors at this stage are likely to have an appreciation of racial and cultural diversity and a commitment to the eradication of oppression within counselling and wider society. During this stage, a non-racist, white, British identity, and an ease around members of culturally different groups, emerges.

White counsellors who are at a place of 'freedom' are those who are most likely to have the ability to facilitate an appropriate therapeutic environment for black clients. Counsellors at a stage of 'conformity', 'conflict', and 'white liberalism' are likely to experience difficulties due to their embracing of a white racist identity.

Black Identity Model

I have adapted below the Minority Identity Models outlined by Adler (1986), Cross (1991, 1995) and Atkinson et al. (1993), in order to address black identity formation in British society.

Conformity

Counsellors and clients are unlikely to see themselves in a cultural and racial way but are likely to have a preference for the values of white British culture. This stage is characterized by down-playing one's own cultural and racial heritage combined with a strong desire to emulate and assimilate white British culture and institutions, along with deprecating attitudes towards self and others in the same cultural and racial group. Counsellors may prefer to work with white clients and can be punitive to black clients. Clients at this stage are likely to hold a preference to work with a white counsellor.

Dissonance – Conflict

There is an increasing acknowledgment of one's own racial and cultural ancestry and an awakening of social-political consciousness. There is a questioning of previous white identification and the beginnings of viewing one's own cultural/racial group positively. Counsellors and clients may experience conflict between appreciation for their own cultural and racial heritage and a desire to conform to white norms. Counsellors may be vulnerable to using the therapeutic process with clients in a voyeuristic way to explore and work through their own feelings about cultural and racial identity.

Realization and immersion – 'Black separatist'

There is a complete surrender to the values of one's own cultural and racial group and a rejection of all non-black values. Counsellors and clients are likely to have a negative attitude towards white culture and be inclined to idealize or romanticize their own cultural and racial group. Typically there is a discomfort with cultural and racial difference and a difficulty in seeing or understanding other oppressions. There is also a preoccupation with judging one's own blackness and other black people to ensure they are being 'black enough'. At this stage shadism would be expressed consciously by a preference for darker skin over light. Derogatory expressions within the black communities such as coconut (meaning black on the outside and white on the inside) and 'Uncle Tom' that are used to describe black people who are not 'black enough' typify this stage. Black counsellors may experience difficulty in forming thera-peutic relationships with white clients. Clients are likely to prefer to see a black counsellor.

Introspection

There is comfort and security in one's own cultural and racial identity and the emergence of an assured black identity. There is a questioning of previ-ous hostility to white culture, white British culture is increasingly under-stood within the context of an historical past and present, and there is likely to be an appreciation and acceptance of some aspects of white culture. Counsellors and clients are likely to use their anger about racial discrimination positively within their own racial social group.

Synergetic articulation & awareness – Freedom

Counsellors and clients have a sense of fulfillment with their own cultural and racial identity and have a positive regard towards themselves and their own cultural and racial group. Cultural and racial identity is likely to be just one important aspect of one's life. There is likely to be a high level of personal autonomy along with an appreciation and respect for other cultural/racial groups. Characteristically, counsellors and clients will have a desire to eliminate all forms of oppression and be inclined to make alliances with members of the dominant culture who are committed to ending oppression and have a sustained commitment to black issues.

Black and white identity models are a useful starting point in making therapeutic assessments about whether it is most appropriate for a client to see a black or white counsellor. They can also help to identify what types of interventions facilitate a client's movement along the model.

Why anti-racism?

Discussion around ethical counselling practices for black clients has often taken place within the ideological framework of multiculturalism. The underlying assumption of multiculturalism is that there is a natural equality between races and cultures and that the way forward is through promoting tolerance of cultural difference. Multiculturalism has been caricatured as 'the three S's: saris, samosas and steel bands' (Carter, 1986). This approach within the field of counselling has resulted in white counsellors being encouraged to acquire cultural knowledge (D'Ardenne & Mahtani, 1999) in order to understand ethnic minority cultures and customs. The danger of this approach is that it encourages generalization about communities and promotes stereotypes at the expense of engaging with the diversity and complexity of black communities and the uniqueness of each individual.

For many black people and white anti-racists the focus of multiculturalism on cultural difference is problematic. The central difficulty is that multiculturalism lacks a structural analysis of racism and consequently has no conceptualization of the structural effects of racism. In reality this results in a focus on cultural practices and differences in isolation, and is divorced from black people's experiences of British racism, which are manifested in structural ways such as inequalities in health, education, housing and employment.

Essentially, within multiculturalism there is no meaningful acknowledgment of the fact that cultural differences in Britain are not viewed within a neutral or value free context but within a dominant context of white supremacy. Multiculturalism's lack of critical analysis renders it, at best, vulnerable to colluding with white supremacy, but at worst, actively promoting it. Focusing attention on black cultures obscures the reality of white racism. Within counselling this can result in a counsellor being pre-occupied with cultural phenomena and detail at the expense of acknowledging a client's experience of oppression or recognizing the counsellor's own collusion with racism.

Without an anti-racist framework, white and black counsellors can fall into various theoretical myths when working with black clients. (Three of these myths are detailed below.)

The colour-blind approach

This approach essentially views issues of race and culture to be an irrelevance, in that all people are viewed as the same. There is no analysis of racism and generally no acknowledgement of its existence. References that a client may make to discrimination or culture are interpreted by the counsellor in an individualistic way, and are viewed as an expression of the client's psychological make up.

Objective/scientific nature of counselling

Within many counselling approaches there is an explicit belief that counselling practice is value free, objective and scientific. This assumption is being increasingly challenged (Chesler, 1989; Fulani, 1988; Greenspan, 1993; Kleinman, 1980); there is a growing recognition that many therapeutic practices reflect the cultural values of a minority of the population. These values are increasingly being identified as patriarchal, middle class, white and heterosexual. Concepts such as neutrality and objectivity within counselling obscure cultural racism and actively promote oppression in society. Assumptions about health and normality within varying counselling approaches well illustrate their cultural bias.

For example:

- Within many counselling approaches clients experiencing visions or hearing voices are generally pathologized and seen as having a medical condition, psychosis. In many cultures experiencing visions or hearing voices are normal every day occurrences and often seen as an indication of spirituality and therefore valued (Okri, 1991).
- Traditionally within western counselling practices, 'normal sexuality' is assumed to be heterosexual, and enforced by the explicit labelling of any other sexuality as deviant.

Pathologizing of black resistance

This occurs when black people's responses to the injustice of racism are viewed *as* the problem, and the causes of their response ignored. bell hooks (1990) argues that black rage and anger should not be seen as pathological or a sign of sickness but as a potentially healthy and healing response to oppression and exploitation. Within a counselling relationship, black clients' expression of anger and pain as a consequence of racist experiences can be interpreted by the counsellor as problematic and a reflection of internal pathology, if not viewed within a wider social and political context. For example, I worked with a black man of Caribbean descent who came to counselling with a psychiatric label of paranoid schizophrenia. In the early stages of counselling, 'Wayne' on many occasions would 'rant' and shout about his experiences of life as a young black man and the atrocities he had endured within the psychiatric system. I found the depth of his pain and anger to be challenging and at times frightening. Although witnessing that pain was uncomfortable, I knew that allowing expression to that rage in a verbal way, within a safe place, was the start of his healing process. Without an anti-racist understanding it might have been easy for me to label Wayne as somebody with anger management difficulties rather than recognizing that his verbal anger was an appropriate response to the injustices that he and other young working class black men experience.

A framework for anti-racist counselling practice

Anti-racist counselling practice can take many forms. Essentially anti-racism is identifiable in that it reflects a belief system that is founded on commitment to social justice. There are several key characteristics that distinguish it from other counselling approaches:

Analysis of racism – structural understanding of society
The foundation of all anti racist models is an understanding and analysis of racism along with an active commitment to eradicate racism within counselling practice and wider society.

Critique of ethnocentrism/cultural racism
This is a critique of the way western counselling traditions have been founded on a particular set of belief systems which reflect the dominant culture, and that these beliefs are invariably capitalistic, patriarchal, and white supremacist and which are assumed to be universal. (See Figure 2.1)

There is also an understanding that conceptions of health and normality are frequently seen as natural or objective states, with no recognition of the way that beliefs about normality or dysfunction are socially constructed. Within anti-racism a critique of ethnocentrism coincides

Rugged Individualism
- Individual is primary unit
- Individual has primary responsibility
- Independence and autonomy highly valued and rewarded
- Individual can control environment

Competition
- Winning is everything
- Win/Lose dichotomy

Action Orientation
- Must master and control nature
- Must always do something about a situation
- Pragmatic /utilitarian view of life

Communication
- Standard English
- Written tradition
- Direct eye contact
- Limited physical contact
- Control of emotions

Time
- Adherence to rigid time
- Time is viewed as a commodity

Holidays
- Based on Christian religion
- Based on white history and male leaders

History
- Based on European experience
- Romanticize war

Protestant Work Ethic
- Working hard brings success

Progress and Future Orientation
- Plan for the future
- Delayed gratification
- Value continual improvement and progress

Emphasis on Scientific Method
- Objective, rational linear thinking
- Cause and effect relationships
- Quantitative emphasis

Status and Power
- Measured by economic possessions
- Credentials, titles, and positions
- Believe 'own' system
- Believe better than other systems
- Owning goods, space, property

Family structure
- Nuclear family is the ideal social unit
- Male is breadwinner and the head of the household
- Female is homemaker and subordinate to the husband
- Patriarchal structure

Aesthetics
- Music and art based on European cultures
- Women's beauty based on blonde, blue-eyed, thin, young
- Men's attractiveness based on athletic ability, power, economic status

Religion
- Belief in Christianity
- No tolerance for deviation from single God concept

Figure 2.1 *White cultural values and beliefs*
Source: Katz (1985)

with a commitment to identify counselling practices that facilitate cultural sensitivity. To promote this, counsellors need to be aware of their own cultural heritage and belief systems along with having an awareness and respect for the client's worldview.

For example, I consider that the adherence to the '50-minute session' a reflection of a western understanding and belief about time (see Figure 2.1). Many clients have difficulty in understanding the rationale for this. Within many counselling traditions there is also a focus and emphasis on the self, and an unquestioned assumption that autonomy and independence are desired states and correspondingly that dependence on and interdependence with others is dysfunctional. The belief that the individual is the primary unit is not universal but particular to some white cultural belief systems.

Similarly, the values placed on the importance of continual improvement and progress, and delayed gratification, evident in some white cultures and reflected in counselling practices, are not shared by all cultures.

Such cultural awareness carries responsibility for not promoting or unwittingly entering into cultural racism or psychological colonization, but of actively developing therapeutic practices, which work with or within the worldview of the client.

Respect for the diversity of black cultures

As well as ensuring that clinical interventions are free from racism, anti-racist counsellors need to be actively acknowledging and respectful of the diversity of black cultures and the achievements of black people. As a counsellor this means knowing that throughout black cultures and history there have been philosophers, scientists, mathematicians, healers, spiritual leaders and artists. If a counsellor lacks this awareness, values of white supremacy and internalized racism are likely to be acted out within the counselling relationship, possibly without a conscious awareness of these dynamics.

Ability to engage with black and white identity issues

Making the decision to become an anti-racist counsellor is not a transition that happens overnight. It is a long and perhaps never-ending journey. Culturally competent counsellors need to aim for 'synergetic articulation' or 'freedom' on the racial/cultural identity models in order to competently identify and address racial and cultural issues in counselling. Within an anti-racist framework there is also a responsibility to identify therapeutic interventions that facilitate the deconstruction of identity formation around values of white supremacy.

Balance between the internal and external world

The conceptualization of structural inequalities within an anti-racist framework is likely to result in a greater emphasis on externalization rather than internalization within the counselling process. I describe externalization in counselling as the process whereby phenomena in society such as oppression and discrimination are connected to clients' personal experiences, thoughts and feelings. Accordingly, I view internalization as the process where the focus is predominantly on a client's feelings, thoughts and behaviours with minimal or no associations to the wider world. Within an anti-racist framework there is an endeavour not to lose sight of the fact that our internal world (i.e. our feelings, sense of self or connection to others, beliefs about the world, conscious and unconscious processes) are greatly influenced by, and a reflection of, the society in which we live. This perspective is likely to facilitate a balance between the internal and external world. Focusing solely on the internal world can render clients vulnerable to labels of medical psychopathology and to be victimized for experiences that have their roots in power inequalties in society.

In summary, an anti-racist framework has direct application for clinical practice in that it provides a theoretical base for the identification and working through of cultural and racial issues in the counselling process. While an anti-racist perspective provides an analysis of the way racism impacts on the lives of black and white people, this in no way diminishes the reality that black people in Britain come from diverse cultural communities and religious backgrounds, and that within black communities there is a complexity of individual experiences which are mediated by a multitude of factors such as age, class, gender, sexuality etc.

Within anti-racism there needs to be an implicit recognition of the diversity and richness of black cultures, along with an explicit value base in the structural analysis of inequalities and an unequivocal and proactive commitment to pathologizing and eradicating racism.

Some guidelines for good practice

This list highlights some key areas and is by no means exhaustive

- Counsellors should have a critical awareness of their own identity and cultural values.
- Counsellors should have an understanding and analysis of racism and an active commitment to the eradication of racism within counselling practice and wider society.

- Counsellors should have respect for and awareness of the diversity of black cultures.
- The identification of a client's cultural values needs to be incorporated into the initial counselling assessment, in order to provide the most culturally appropriate counselling intervention.
- Counsellors should be aware of the use of black and white identity models as a tool for the identification of cultural and racial issues in counselling.
- Externalization of social inequalities: the counselling process should facilitate integration between clients' internal world and wider society, in order to minimize the process whereby clients are 'blamed' and held responsible for experiencing inequalities such as racism.
- The inclusion of race and cultural issues should be an integral part of all counselling training.

Notes

1 Black – I use the word in the political sense to denote:

    a. A shared history of colonization, imperialism, slavery, racism and the general legacy of the Diaspora

    b. History of collective solidarity and resistance against colonization, imperialism, slavery, genocide and white supremacy

2 Racism – is used as a short hand way of categorizing the systematic mistreatment that 'black' people experience in Britain and around the world. In using the word I do not wish to support the contention that there are biologically distinct races.

References

Adams, M.V. (1996) *The Multicultural Imagination 'Race', Colour and the Unconscious.* London and New York: Routledge.

Adler, N.J. (1986) 'Cultural Synergy: Managing the Impact of Cultural Diversity', in *1986 Annual: Development Human Resources.* San Diego, CA: University Associates.

Akbar, N. (1984) *Chains & Images of Psychological Slavery.* Jersey City, NJ: New Minds Publication.

Atkinson, D.R., Morten, G. & Sue, D.W. (1993) *Counselling American Minorities.* Dubuque, IA: Brown & Benchmark.

Balarajan, R. (1991) in T. Modood & R. Berthoud (eds) (1997) *Ethnic Minorities in Britain: Diversity & Disadvantage.* London: Policy Studies Institute.

Carter, S. (1998) *Hidden Crisis: A Study of Black and Minority Homelessness in London.* London: Frontline Housing Agency.

Carter, T. (1986) *Shattering Illusions: West Indians in British Politics.* London: Lawrence & Wishart.

Chesler, P. (1989) *Women and Madness.* London: Harcourt Brace Jovanovich.

Commission for Racial Equality (1997) *Employment and Unemployment.* Fact Sheet. London: Commission for Racial Equality.

Commission for Racial Equality (1999) *Criminal Justice in England and Wales.* Fact Sheet. London: Commission for Racial Equality.

Commission for Racial Equality. (1999) *Housing and Homelessness.* Fact Sheet. London: Commission for Racial Equality.

Cross, W.E. (1991) *Shades of Black: Diversity in African American Identity.* Philadelphia, PA: Temple University Press.

Cross W.E. (1995) 'The Psychology of Nigresence: Revising the Cross Model', in J.G. Ponterotto, J.M. Casas, L.A. Suzuki & C.M. Alexander (eds), *Handbook of Multicultural Counselling One.* Thousand Oaks, CA: Sage.

D'Ardenne, P. & Mahtani, A. (1999) *Transcultural Counselling in Action.* London: Sage.

Davis, A. (1983) *Women Race and Class.* New York: Vintage.

Dominelli, L. (1998) *Anti-Racist Social Work. A Challenge for White Practitioners and Educators.* London: Macmillan.

Fanon, F. (1963) *The Wretched of the Earth.* New York: Grove.

Fanon, F. (1967) *Black Skin, White Masks.* New York: Grove.

Fernando, S. (1991) *Mental Health Race and Culture.* London: Macmillan.

Fulani, L. (ed.) (1988) *The Psychopathology of Everyday Racism and Sexism.* London: Harrington Park Press.

Gordon, L.R. (ed.) (1997) *Existence in Black: An Anthology of Black Existential Philosophy.* London: Routledge.

Greenspan, M. (1993) *A New Approach to Women and Therapy.* New York: McGraw-Hill.

Helms, J.E. (1984) 'Toward a Theoretical Model of the Effects of Race on Counselling: A Black and White Model.' *Counselling Psychologist,* 12, 153–65.

Holland, S. (1990) 'Psychotherapy, Oppression and Social Action: Gender, Race and Class in Black Women's Depression', in R.J. Perelberg & A.C. Miller (ed.), *Gender and Power* in *Families.* London: Routledge.

Home Office (1997) *Prison Statistics: England and Wales.* London: HMSO.

Home Office (1998b) *Prison Statistics: England and Wales.* London: HMSO.

hooks, bell (1990) *Yearning: Race, Gender and Cultural Politics.* Boston: South End Press.

hooks, bell (1996) *Killing Rage: Ending Racism.* London: Penguin

Jackson, A.M. (2000) 'Shadism: the Psychological Hangover of Slavery.' *Counselling,* II(9).

Kamalu, C. (1990) *Foundations of African Thought: A Worldview Grounded in the African Heritage of Religion, Philosophy, Science and Art.* London: Karnac.

Kareem, J. & Littlewood, R. (1992) *Intercultural Therapy: Themes, Interpretations and Practice.* Oxford: Blackwell Scientific Publications.

Katz, J. (1985) 'The Sociopolitical Nature of Counselling.' *Counselling Psychologist,* 13, 615–24.

Kleinman, A. (1980) *Patients and Healers in the Context of Culture: An Exploration of the Borderline between Anthropology, Medicine & Psychiatry.* London: University of California Press.

Laing, R.D. (1962) *The Divided Self.* London: Pelican.

Lipsky, S (1998) 'Internalised Oppression.' *RC Journal Black Re-emergence,* 2.

Lorde, A. (1984) *Sister Outsider.* New York: Crossing Press.

Macpherson, W. (1999) *The Stephen Lawrence Inquiry.* London: HMSO.

Marx, K. & Engels, F. (1968) *The Marx/Engels Selected Works.* Vol. I. London: Lawrence and Wishart.

MIND (1993) *Minds Policy on Black and Ethnic Minority People and Mental Health Policy.* Mind File. Policy 1.

Modood, T., Berthoud, R., Lakey, J., Nazroo, J., Smith, P., Virdee, S. and Beishon, S. (1997) *Ethnic Minorities in Britain, Diversity and Disadvantage.* London: Policy Studies Institute.

Moodley, P. & Perkins, R. (1990) 'Blacks and Psychiatry: A Framework for Understanding Access to Psychiatric Services'. *Bulletin of the Royal College of Psychiatrists*, 14.

Nazroo, J.Y. (1998) *The Health of Britain's Ethnic Minorities: Findings from a National Survey.* London: Policy Studies Institute.

Okri, B. (1991) *The Famished Road.* London: Vintage.

Ratcliffe, P. (1996) *Race and Housing in Bradford.* Bradford: Housing Forum.

Smith, B. (1999) P*otency, Permission, Protection and Politics.* ITA News, 17–20.

Sue, D.W. & Sue, D. (1999) *Counselling the Culturally Different: Theory and Practice.* New York: John Wiley.

Sue, G. (ed.) (1998) *Multicultural Counseling Competencies Individual and Organisational Development.* Thousand Oaks, CA: Sage.

Wallace, M. (1979) *Black Macho and the Myth of Superwomen.* New York: Dial.

Williams, E. (1981) *Capitalism and Slavery.* London: Andre Deutsch.

Wren, C.G. (1962) 'The Culturally Encapsulated Counsellor'. *Harvard Educational Review*, 32.

3   *Developing Anti-disabling Counselling Practice*

Mairian Corker

> Becoming disabled brings us into some odd relationships with people. One that most of us are familiar with is the doctor–patient relationship. When we're in it, we play a role, the sick role. We're expected to play it whether we're sick or not. Most of us know that it is in our interests to play it – we've never been taught the lines, but we soon catch up on what we're supposed to say. (Davis, 1993: 197)

This chapter aims to encourage counsellors to move towards an understanding of disabled people as an oppressed group, and counselling as a potentially oppressive process. In this context it is important to note that disabled people are now 'protected' by anti-discriminatory legislation in relation to service provision, and service provision includes counselling (The Disability Discrimination Act, 1995). But there are many ways in which this 'protection' differs considerably from that accorded to women and people from different ethnic and cultural backgrounds. The most important difference is that it is the view of politicians, their advisors – indeed, of society at large – that there are no fundamental disabling belief and value systems embedded in society's institutions that are equivalent to those perpetuated through racism and sexism. In other words, discrimination against disabled people is *not* seen to be institutionalized. The second main difference is that disabled people have to prove they are disabled before they can use the Act to make a claim, and the proof has to be given in ways that are prescribed by law. Part of the reason for this may be that when a society believes that it 'cares' for and makes provision for the welfare of a particular group of people, it also tends to believe that it cannot be oppressive towards that group of people. Nevertheless, this chapter, building on the perspectives of disabled counsellors and clients, will suggest that such perspectives may be misguided.

The chapter aims primarily to encourage the reader to examine the philosophical basis of their notions of counselling (van Deurzen-Smith, 1988), of the person (Corker, 1998; McLeod, 1993) and of disability, and how they might interact to influence counselling practice in different ways. This approach is one that gets comparatively little attention in an increasingly skills-based counselling literature, in spite of the recognition of the importance of unconscious processes to counselling practice. The various 'toolkits' described by this literature seem overly methodological, encouraging counsellors to move away from self-reflection. Further, there is no doubt in my mind that these toolkits have stimulated the movement of counselling 'techniques' and 'technologies' into many institutional domains where they would not otherwise have been present, and where they have been restructured in the service of institutional power (Fairclough, 1992). This is critical for all those who experience institutionalized oppression. But it is particularly important for disabled people because it means that the view that we are 'perpetual clients' in our relationships with non-disabled professionals, as described by Ken Davis in the opening quotation, is not confined to the institution of medicine.

While reading this chapter it is important to bear in mind that disabled people are a very diverse group, and the differences between us have very significant theoretical and practical implications for counselling. A short chapter such as this cannot in any way do justice to this diversity and at the same time accord proper recognition to the fact that, in describing the field of anti-discriminatory counselling practice, disability does not begin from a level playing field. Whereas there are many texts that deal specifically with counselling practice relating to other areas of social inequality, this is generally not so for disability. Existing examples, such as Corker (1994, 1996); Lenny (1993); Marks (2000); Oliver, J. (1995); Olkin (1999); Reeve (2000); Segal (1989); Swain (1995); and Withers (1996), tend to be written from a wide variety of practical and theoretical perspectives.

What is disability?

I have set the scene for this chapter by describing 'disabled people' as an oppressed group, and through use of the pronouns 'we' and 'our', I have signified that I am a part of that group. Being 'part of' this group means two things. It means first that I acknowledge the collective nature of social discrimination and its negative consequences for disabled people in all aspects of our everyday lives. But perhaps more importantly it signifies that I identify with the affirmative political identity, promoted by the disabled people's movement, which seeks to oppose this discrimination through the removal of disabling barriers to disabled people's participation in society, and through the development of anti-discriminatory philosophy and practice. In the context of counselling, this means, for example, that I see counselling as having a political dimension and counselling practice as a *potential* force for the emancipation of disabled people. This position reflects the 'social model of disability', which was conceived from within, and is used by the disabled people's movement (Oliver, 1996; Barnes, Mercer and Shakespeare, 1999).

In Britain, the social model makes a conceptual distinction between *impairment* on the one hand, and *disability* on the other, in a way that is similar to the feminist distinction between sex and gender. Disability is then described as institutionalized barriers that work to exclude disabled people from, or discriminate against disabled people in the mainstream of economic and social life. Examples of barriers that may discriminate in the counselling setting include:

- The physical characteristics of counselling settings (the counselling, counselling supervision or counselling training environment) that prevent access;
- Socially and/or professionally entrenched belief and value systems (world views) about counselling, disabled people and disability in the counsellor's and the client's unconscious;
- The way in which these world views filter through into the attitudes expressed in different counselling settings and the forms of counselling practice in which counsellors engage when working with disabled clients.

For an interesting example of the social model in relation to people with 'madness and distress' (which is the term used by survivors of the mental health system), see Beresford (2000).

At the same time, counsellors who work mostly with individual clients may have some difficulty in reconciling a model that relates to a group of people with their focus on the individual, especially when ideas about groups tend not to be inclusive of everyone. It helps to have a way of talking about difference *within* the category 'disability' that is meaningful for the individual but doesn't fall into the trap of *stereotyping* them as 'disabled' or 'not disabled'. This is especially important as the concept of disability unites a heterogeneous group of people whose only commonality, as we will see below, is being perceived as not 'normal'. It also means that disability is a transient category that is very different to 'race' and gender for example – most people are not born disabled. Within the social model, impairment refers to physical, sensory and cognitive/intellectual characteristics that make people with impairments different from people without impairments. That is to say living in society as a blind person, for example, is different to living in society as a sighted person when society is designed only for sighted people. Equally, a society that is designed for wheelchair users will often make very little direct difference to a blind person or a person with learning difficulties, because that society will be accustomed to dividing disabled people up in terms of their impairments. A useful way to think about this is that the population of disabled people consists of different impairment 'cultures' – where 'culture' is understood as a way of life. At the same time, structural factors impact on *all* people with impairments in ways that work against our recognition as 'cultural beings'.

This dual approach is important because conventional ways of understanding disability are framed by the *'individual'* or *'medical' models*. These models assume impairment to be the cause of *all* the difficulties experienced by individual disabled people, and they often conflate impairment (for example hearing, visual, speech and mobility impairment) and illness (for example multiple sclerosis, chronic fatigue syndrome, HIV/AIDS). Though impairment may occasionally be accompanied by chronic or spasmodic episodes of illness and/or pain that lead to periods of severe emotional and psychological distress, it certainly is not always the case. Equally, as people with impairments, we can be emotionally or mentally distressed in ways that have nothing to do with our impairments, or with disability (French, 1994).

But even when impairment or chronic illnesses are not visible, there is a tendency to stereotype disabled people in ways that suggest they *are* their impairments. Thus we are perceived as sick, tragic, incompetent, dependent, incomplete *per se* and, importantly for the purposes of counselling, to be in need of rehabilitation, cure or care to help us to 'normalize' or feel better about ourselves, *whether this matches our own perception or not*. Disabled people who have visible impairments compound this way of thinking because it can be hard to look beyond what we actually see – we see the impairment and not the person.

In summary, the difference between the individual/medical models and the social model, is that the former marks people with impairments as being *inferior* to, and 'abnormal' when compared with, 'normal' people, whereas the latter marks us as different and doesn't make value judgements of this kind. The characteristics of the two models of disability – 'individual' and 'social' – are summarized and analysed in Oliver (1996) and Barnes et al. (1999), and I would urge readers to look to these sources because they give more detail than I can give here, and provide extensive reading lists. However, it must be stressed that these models are frameworks for *thinking about* disability, but they do not necessarily allow us to *understand* disability as it relates to diverse individual experiences. In this context, I would suggest that it is not useful to take *any* model for granted.

What is disabling practice?

Though disabled people have for almost three decades been describing what they mean by discriminatory practice, the Disability Discrimination Act 1995 is still very young in comparison to other kinds of anti-discrimination legislation and so the proof is not yet in the pudding. Thus, there is no 'official' body of case law describing discriminatory counselling practice, and the absence of this 'official stamp' means that it is quite difficult for disabled people to convince non-disabled counsellors that they discriminate, let alone describe how they discriminate. This is in itself a measure of how powerful certain stereotypes of disability are. Nevertheless, where the social model is of great value for describing both discriminatory and anti-discriminatory counselling practice in relation to disabled people, is in the way it allows us to think about counsellors, as providers of 'helping' and 'welfare' services, as being potentially part of disabling society. As such, counselling may become part of the social creation of disablement.

I will now turn to some common examples of the kinds of barriers that were described in the previous section. But in so doing, I want to emphasize that disabled people generally seek counselling or wish to become counsellors for exactly the same range of reasons as non-disabled people. Additionally, for some of us, the desire to become a counsellor is directly related to our knowledge, gleaned from the stories disabled people have told us of how existing counselling practice discriminates. Further, many of these stories are from disabled people who come to counselling with a history of abusive 'helping' situations, where we have not have been listened to, let alone understood. For example:

> 'Do you really expect us to believe that anyone could want to have sex with a smelly, shitty child like you?' If a (defence) lawyer can speak this way to a

disabled child in the witness box at their abuse trial, where can we turn to block out the din?

'This is probably part of some rare syndrome.' If a doctor can write this on the case notes of a disabled girl on whose body he has just noted anal and vaginal tearing and bruising, where can we turn to heal our wounds? (Cross, 1994: 163)

After Mrs Z was widowed, the doctor advised: 'Don't tell your son.' She had enough problems. 'He might make more problems for you, and anyway he won't understand.' Acting on his advice Mrs Z kept the death of her husband secret for several months and merely told her mentally handicapped [sic] son that father had 'gone away'. It was a dreadful strain for her, grieving for her husband and at the same time having to keep the death secret from her adult son who was sharing the same house. When she finally did tell him, she discovered that he had known for some weeks, and felt very resentful that she had not talked about it to him before. He had somehow found out from things he had overheard at the day centre. (Oswin, 1990)

Ideological and attitudinal barriers

Ideological barriers, as we have seen, are of three kinds that relate to fundamental beliefs about counselling, the person and disability. Ideology and attitudes are transmitted through language, both verbal and non-verbal, in our relationships with others. The language that counsellors use will send particular and not always intended messages to disabled clients regarding what they think and/or know about disability. For example, using the term 'people with disabilities' may be offensive to some disabled people, whereas other disabled people are happy with the term 'crip'. Some may prefer the term 'impairment', as in 'hearing impaired', and others may view it with disdain. Yet others refuse both 'disability' and 'impairment' because they are labels that distract from the person. Language is also accompanied by particular forms of behaviour that may be interpreted differently within different impairment cultures. For example, attentiveness can be interpreted as staring by someone with a physical impairment, but a lack of attentiveness can be insulting to someone who is deaf. There is no rule of thumb in relation to language use. Being preoccupied with semantics, or indeed with how much one claims to 'know' about a particular impairment, can make counselling process stilted and difficult for the disabled client. What is important is to listen to the language that individual disabled people use in different counselling settings and to reflect this language in interaction, until such time as it is appropriate to change the language, in challenging or confronting internalized and unhelpful self-perceptions, for example.

In self-reflexive practice, language can be adjusted relatively easily. But it is more commonly when discriminatory beliefs and values in relation to disabled people and disability become bound up in counselling values and process that difficulties can arise. Indeed it is unsurprising that this happens when we consider the authority of some of counselling and psychotherapy's 'root metaphors':

> ... the different root metaphors, images or basic assumptions about reality which underlie different approaches to counselling can make it difficult or impossible to reconcile or combine certain approaches ... [counsellors are] immersed in these cultural images, as well as being socialized into the language and ideology of a particular counselling approach or into the implicit norms and values of a counselling agency. (McLeod, 1993:19–20)

Influential examples include Freud's belief that 'the ego wears an auditory lobe' and his hierarchical oppositions between 'normal'/pathological, conscious/unconscious, sane/insane, real/imaginary, experience/dream and masculine/feminine, and Lacan's inscription of speech as the 'discourse of truth'. All of these root metaphors reflect and play into common disablist stereotypes, and may be internalized by counsellors. As such, there is a risk that they will be projected onto disabled clients in the counselling relationship. Counsellors working within these different traditions need to ask, for example:

- Where 'inarticulate' clients, clients with learning difficulties and clients with language and communication impairments are located within Lacan's 'discourse of truth';
- How these metaphors might impact on perspectives of some disabled people's 'ability' to train as counsellors;
- What might be the impact of the need for language mediation on issues of confidentiality, and
- How might disabled people's sexuality be viewed within Freudian oppositions?

But it is also critical to recognize that impairment cultures can strike right at the heart of these metaphors in ways that lead counsellors to act defensively and, therefore, oppressively. For example, consider these comments by Dan (not his real name), a counselling trainee who is blind:

Dan

> Almost everything I have tried to do regarding the inclusion of visual impairment and disability on my training course has been ignored, blocked or oppressed. At one point I was strongly advised to leave the course and deal with my 'personal problems' in therapy ... ironic don't you think? While they emphasized my difficulty in processing information and suggested that I was

not sufficiently reflexive, they just didn't seem to be able to grasp that as a visually impaired person, unable to read printed text, I might just process information differently, albeit in ways that challenged how they 'normally' delivered the course. Their own lack of self-reflection prevents them from understanding that my 'personal problems' might just stem from their lack of support, lack of awareness of disability issues, lack of empathic understanding. All that is without their own projected fears of blindness and inherent uncertainties that created their anxieties about my difference. I certainly don't get the same support as other trainees either in terms of quantity or in terms of quality. Instead, this lack becomes my deficiency. I am labelled as not showing the right attitude or having sufficient humility to succeed as a counsellor. I wonder precisely what they mean by 'right' and whether 'humility' could be replaced by acquiescence?

To Dan's comment, it might be added that attitudes like those he experienced are perhaps the most significant obstacle to the promotion of anti-disabling counselling practice. By putting disabled people 'out of sight' in the training context, they put different understandings of disability 'out of mind', preventing these understandings from becoming integral to the profession.

Disabling identity
There are also very powerful metaphors that concern the experience of disability and its relationship to personal, social and political identity. One example is the view that all disabled people are *dependent*. Obviously, some of us are not able to go about our daily lives without support (personal assistance, technical and auxiliary aids, or medication) and for many of us, the level of support that we have is controlled by available resources and not by our needs. But sometimes we feel forced to rely on 'support' when we don't want it and so we exist in a state of 'hostile dependency'. For example, some deaf people become demoralized with constantly using a third party to mediate communication because it prevents communication difficulties being addressed directly. The important thing about perceptions of dependency, however, is that they can feed into notions that disabled people are 'childlike' and 'powerless' and so we are often treated like children. Indeed, because disabled children are assumed to match the traditional view of children as passive, incompetent and incomplete, and are therefore perceived to be the responsibility of non-disabled adults, there are many ways in which disabled adults are compelled to live in a state of perpetual childhood. It is because of these stereotypes that the comment 'But you speak so well!' to a deaf person, for example, can cause a storm in the psychic landscape.

Another metaphor that is commonly assumed is that the experience of *loss or lack* is central to disabled people's experience. And, as Withers

(1996: 103) notes, 'many counsellors believe that any loss, whether through the death of a person, loss of a faculty or loss of a body function, needs to be mourned'. We will return to loss and lack in more detail below, but the centrality of this experience is commonly linked to the widespread belief that to be disabled is to have a 'negative self-identity'. Counselling then becomes a process of helping us towards a more 'positive' world-view. This is something of a double-edged sword not least because 'positivity' and 'negativity' are ultimately subjective value judgements. On the one hand, accepting one's impairment may also mean accepting that one has 'weaknesses', real or perceived, and this can be generalized to the self as a whole in such a way that it becomes consistent with an unhelpful self-perception. On the other, using the counselling process to build an 'affirmative identity' may pressurize some clients with hidden impairments to 'come out' before they are ready or willing to do so. It can also persuade clients to engage in a narcissistic pursuit of a Utopia that doesn't exist in order to avoid the distressing aspects of their lives (Craib, 1994; 1998). This can result in the acquisition of a false consciousness that doesn't stand up to scrutiny in the disabled person's everyday life, and is inconsistent with their experience of oppression.

Within counselling practice, a focus on *either* a 'negative identity' *or* a 'positive identity' has two main effects. First, it can complicate the relationship between counselling process and the balance of power in the counselling relationship, in a way that prevents counselling practice from meeting goals that are truly client-centred. Second, such a focus all too frequently reinforces the individual/medical model's assumption that people *are* their impairments or their experience of disability. Though a 'struggle over identity' is frequently on the agenda when disabled clients seek counselling and the questions 'who am I?' and 'where do I belong?' are central to this struggle (Corker, 1996; Withers, 1996), this struggle is not always concerned with impairment and disability. For example, though I have said that I am a disabled person, disabled people are not the only oppressed group to which I belong. I am also a woman and a lesbian and I was once a disabled child, which emphasizes that my life experience is complex and multi-dimensional. In matters of 'who I am', the physical fact of my deafness is inconsequential when compared to the social impact of living in a society that cannot deal with personal complexity and 'deviance'. (For further examples of the different ways in which disabled people talk about these issues, see Corker and French, 1999, and also the second case study below.) It is helpful here to consider that notions about what is 'negative' or 'affirmative' are sometimes themselves projections of parts of ourselves that we reject or cherish, but these projections may be incompatible with someone else's psychic or social landscape.

Physical barriers to accessing counselling

For many disabled people, physical barriers to access emerge well before any other barriers simply because they come before the counselling relationship can be established. Physical barriers include characteristics of the physical environment, for example:

- Bright or dim lighting (people with hearing and visual impairments);
- Type of furniture (people with arthritis);
- Width of doorways, stairs (wheelchair users, and people with heart disease);
- Entry-phones (deaf people and people with restricted growth);
- Information (disabled people from different cultural or ethnic backgrounds, deaf people, people with learning difficulties);
- Face-to-face contact (some people with autism); and
- Economic barriers (most disabled people live on or near the poverty line).

These barriers will be more pronounced in private practice, which, though it tends to be more diverse in its provision, is also expensive, relies heavily on self-referral, and is more likely to be based in the counsellor's own home.

But we also have to think of disability in terms of the *indirect* consequences of these barriers. Certainly, their existence means that disabled people have more limited choice, and, when they manifest themselves as barriers to training, this can mean that disabled clients do not have access to disabled counsellors, even when this is what they would prefer. For some this will mean having to work with a counsellor they don't feel comfortable with because that is better than no counsellor at all. Others may be forced to approach familiar or 'free' sources of help or information – commonly NHS primary care services – which may place limitations on the approaches to counselling that are on offer and the settings in which it takes place.

Towards anti-disablist practice

It is only when counsellors have sought to identify and remove ideological, physical, and discursive and attitudinal barriers to disabled people's access to and participation in counselling (whether as clients or providers, trainees or trainers, supervisees or supervisors) that counselling practice can be regarded as anti-discriminatory. It would be easy to spend the rest of this chapter focusing on the removal of physical barriers. However, such a focus, in my view, is the main drawback of so-called 'disability awareness' training for counsellors, especially when it is carried out by non-disabled people who have limited experience of disability or counselling. Further, it is difficult to see the value of this focus if what is being accessed – that is, counselling itself – has not sought to rid itself of inherently disabling practice. I therefore find it more helpful to view counselling as a discursive activity, as relationship-bound (Woolfe and Sugarman, 1989), and as potentially complicit in the social construction of disability (McLeod, 1997):

> There is ... a strong commitment to viewing the therapeutic encounter as a milieu for the creative generation of meaning. The client's voice is not merely an auxiliary device for the vindication of the therapist's pre-determined narrative, but serves in these contexts as an essential constituent of a jointly constructed reality ... The emphasis, then, is on the collaborative relationship between client and therapist as they strive to develop forms of narrative that may usefully enable the client to move beyond the current or continuing crisis. (Gergen and Kaye, 1992: 174–5)

Because, as McLeod suggests, 'we do not live in a social world which is dominated by a unitary, all-encompassing sets of ideas' (1993: 19), to consciously or unconsciously impose such a set of ideas, whatever its frame of reference, is what constitutes discriminatory practice in counselling.

I now want to turn to two concrete examples of work with disabled clients that illustrate some of the challenges of working with disabled people in a social climate where stereotyped views of disability and/or human experience are commonplace. The first example is taken from the experience of a disabled counsellor who wishes to remain anonymous.

Sally

> I am involved in a counselling relationship with Sally, who is in her twenties and has Asperger's syndrome (which is a form of autism). We work by typing everything into a computer because face-to-face contact makes her shut off. When I first met her, I had no idea how to be with her, until I read an autobiography of somebody with autism, which has given me a base at least. After a couple of years of working together, she has decided she is a lesbian, because she feels such affection and has fantasies in connection with a Japanese lesbian cartoon character. Virtually all of her social life is comprised of what, for me, are 'imaginary worlds and characters'. I have to keep reminding myself that, for her, they are real. As she was telling me about her realization, I became

concerned because she had described her parents, with whom she lives, as very conservative and religious. I am lesbian, and began to worry inside about some kind of lawsuit if she 'comes out' to them, and this got in the way of my listening. So I asked her, 'How can you know about your sexual orientation if you have never had sex, and have this crush on an imaginary character?' She commented: 'Well … couldn't that be said of all of us in some ways?' I was stunned, and annoyed at myself, and really could only agree.

There are many parts to this example, but it seems mainly to be about what happens when worlds, and world-views, collide in the counselling room. It is tempting, as Donna did, to divide up these worlds into 'real' (her world) and 'imaginary' (Sally's world). The 'real' world, for Donna, is one in which 'conservative and religious' people may be, or perhaps are, homophobic and, it should be added, one that seems to reduce sexual orientation to sexual practice. We are not told whether Sally 'knows' Donna is a lesbian, nor what Donna means by 'lesbian'. But given that Sally is in her twenties, there may also be a fear on Donna's part that the parents regard Sally as a perpetual child, and disabled at that, with whom, like the child described by Cross above, 'no-one would want to have sex'. How, then, can she 'know about her sexual orientation'. Donna's unconscious world 'gets in the way of her listening' and she momentarily forgets that 'real' and 'imaginary' are stereotypes that people with autism often challenge. Indeed, some people with autism become sexually aroused by material objects, and 'people' do not, therefore, enter into their understanding of sexuality. At the same time, since Donna can only 'know' Sally's parents through Sally herself, how can she position her fears in relation to them as 'real' or 'imaginary' any more than she can describe Sally's world as 'imaginary' and hers as 'real'? Though Donna had let go of Sally's 'reality', Sally ended up demonstrating just how in touch with Donna's 'real' world she was.

The second example is taken from my own work, which was primarily with deaf people. The deaf population represents a particular challenge to ideas about what constitutes anti-disabling practice. This issue is too complex to consider fully here, but, in general, counsellors must move away from understanding deafness as the (in)ability to hear (the medical model) and towards deafness as linguistic and cultural diversity[1].

Jennifer

I worked with Jennifer for over two years. She was in her 50s, divorced, and became deaf suddenly twenty years ago. She communicated orally but did not lip-read well and had only rudimentary knowledge of sign language. The issues she brought to counselling were: the difficulty she had with continuing relationships with hearing people; the loneliness that came from the loss of her youngest child – her main source of support – who had moved away from home; and her anger about the bias and uncaring attitude of different helping services, which she felt were giving priority to deaf people who used sign language.

Three months into the relationship, Jennifer said to me 'I want to be hearing.' I felt it was important to clarify exactly what she meant by this statement, and her response turned out to be complex: 'I want to be who I am and I want my hearing friends to remember that though I am physically and functionally different, I am still me, I still have a hearing experience. I'm not bothered about being deaf but I am bothered about the tinnitus that wears me out, and the fact that because I'm deaf, old friends think that I've changed – that I'm no longer a feminist, no longer the political animal I've always been. I sometimes feel as if I am constantly having to justify myself … constantly fighting for the right to continue to be who I am.'

What Jennifer was saying was that she accepted who she was, including the deaf part of herself. Her experience of disability came from expectations placed on her to conform to the common stereotype of deafened people and assumptions that her deafness must be the most important aspect of her life. She later said, 'I wouldn't experience being deaf at all if they allowed me to continue being who I am. Really, the deafness belongs to them.'

Hillary Ratna (1996: 240) feels, reflecting much of the literature that abounds on the subject, that work with deafened people requires 'an [essential] understanding of bereavement and loss issues'. My experiences with clients like Jennifer made me rather more cautious, because for her, disability (in the social model sense), power and control were significant issues. She never conveyed feelings of loss except in the sense of 'losing' her youngest son, which had precipitated a renewed attention to her disabled life and the lack of support she received. It may well be the case that *all* counsellors need some understanding of these issues, irrespective of the client group they work with. But this must be accompanied by an awareness that loss itself, and the response to it, can be stereotyped in a way that appears to collude with the medical/individual model of disability.

For example, many theories of loss suggest that to experience loss, we must first experience *having* the person or the thing that is lost. Hence, it is frequently assumed that people who are born with impairments, and have never experienced anything other than a disabled lifestyle do not experience loss of hearing, sight or mobility, for example. Many deaf people living in hearing families refer to very strong childhood feelings of difference and of 'something missing' and recall very acute memories of seeing the emotional and non-verbal response of their parents and siblings to sound, though not fully understanding what was provoking that response. They remember questioning internally why they were not part of that response. When they noticed, again through seeing changes in emotional colour and tone, that hearing children were part of the response they interpreted this difference in terms of feeling left out and 'lost'. The uncritical use of a 'bereavement model' might have resulted in Jennifer's original comment '*I want to be hearing*' being interpreted that she missed being hearing and was not able to accept being deaf which, in turn, might have obstructed the growth process.

Much of the subsequent work I did with Jennifer focused on how she perceived herself using images – a prominent one being that of a turtle encased in a tough carapace and with a strong beak which protected her against the diminution of her sense of herself. But she became aware that the snapping beak also symbolized the way she communicated with important people in her life, because she needed to keep a sense of control, and had difficulty with 'letting go of someone she had caught'. It was important for me to accept that her understanding of communication referred to how meaning was built up in her relations with others and not about what language she did or didn't use. We used the counselling relationship to explore alternative and clearer ways of communicating and, after a time, her images became 'softer' as she became strong enough within to allow herself to express her vulnerabilities.

Concluding remarks

Whilst models and frameworks of counselling, disabled people and disability are useful tools in helping us to think about the process of counselling, they can restrict client growth if they are applied too rigorously, and without a critical awareness of their limits. They can also operate at an unconscious level, entering into the counselling relationship when we don't expect them to. The social model of disability is often neglected in counselling work with disabled people. Yet it reminds us that the counsellor–client relationship is rarely an equal one, and the counsellor, as the power holder in most therapeutic relationships, is responsible for the safety and containment of the therapeutic environment. How this environment is constructed can produce client empowerment as much as it can reinforce client oppression and add to the experience of being disabled.

It is worth remembering that, although notoriously difficult to measure, the 'success' of therapy seems to depend to a large degree on how the counsellor is perceived by the client. Counsellors working with disabled clients might in general learn far more from the processes of self-reflection and unconditional engagement with their clients' world views, than from absorbing the various 'definitive', stereotyped and delimiting accounts of disability and of therapy as a 'talking cure'. These accounts can hide the uniqueness of individuals and individual therapeutic relationships. When we consider anti-discriminatory practice in work with disabled people, it is in some ways a very deep irony that counselling is, from the client's perspective, very much a case of 'see the person, not the disability'. For, as counsellors, we have to acknowledge that it is often *us* who are the disability. Counselling that constantly builds or plays upon a person's *perceived* weakness or disadvantage cannot be called therapeutic. But nor can counselling that assumes that the answer to disabled people's problems is that they accept a state of false consciousness, however affirmative it may seem.

Key points for good practice:

- Disabled people are a very diverse group, and this diversity has very significant theoretical and practical implications for counselling.
- Counselling has a political dimension and counselling practice must be viewed as a *potential* force for social change.
- When working with disabled people, counsellors need to examine the 'root metaphors' of counselling, of the person *and of disability*, with particular reference to how they might interact to influence counselling practice in different ways.
- Two key root metaphors for understanding disability are those that view disability as a problem that resides in the individual (the medical/individual model), and those that see disability as socially created barriers that are imposed on individuals (the social model). However, the former is institutionalized.
- When working with disabled clients, the success of counselling may depend on the extent to which counsellors are self-reflexive in their attention to and removal of ideological, physical, discursive and attitudinal barriers, and their preparedness to listen to and accept what different clients mean by disability.

Notes

1 There are three parallel elements to this diversity. First, people with hearing impairments may use spoken language or sign language, or a combination of the two. Second,

each of these language groups can be thought of as representing different communities. Thus people with hearing impairments tend to form dominant social affiliations on the basis of language choices. And finally, deaf education continues to be split between residential schools and mainstream schools, and the quality of deaf education varies enormously on a geographical basis. Therefore educational factors tend to play a significant role in the language choices and community affiliations eventually made by adults with hearing impairments, and also in the skill with which different languages are used. It is not always possible, nor is it advisable to try to fit people with hearing impairments into discrete groups defined on the basis of these three parameters. There is nevertheless one group that does present itself as separate from the others: namely, the *Deaf* community. People who are Deaf currently constitute a very small minority within the wider disabled population, and, though they come within the DDA's definition of disability, the community tends to reject the idea that Deaf people are disabled (see Corker, 1994, 1996, 1998). It is for this reason that I have not sought to over-emphasize my work with this group within the context of this chapter.

References

Barnes, C., Mercer, G. & Shakespeare, T. (1999) *Exploring Disability: A Sociological Introduction*. Cambridge: Polity.

Beresford, P. (2000) 'What have Madness and Psychiatric System Survivors got to do with Disability and Disability Studies? *Disability & Society*, 15(1), pp. 167–72.

Corker, M. (1994) *Counselling – The Deaf Challenge*. London: Jessica Kingsley.

Corker, M. (1996) *Deaf Transitions*. London: Jessica Kingsley.

Corker, M. (1998) *Deaf and Disabled or Deafness Disabled*. Buckingham: Open University Press.

Corker, M. and French, S. (1999) *Disability Discourse*. Buckingham: Open University Press.

Craib, I. (1994) *The Importance of Disappointment*. London: Routledge.

Craib, I. (1998) *Experiencing Identity*. London: Sage.

Cross, M. (1994) 'Abuse', in L. Keith (ed.), *Mustn't Grumble*. London: The Women's Press, pp. 163–66.

Davis, K. (1993) 'The Crafting of Good Clients', in J. Swain, V. Finkelstein, S. French & M. Oliver (eds), *Disabling Barriers – Enabling Environments*. London: Sage, in association with the Open University, pp. 197–200.

Eisenberg, G. (1996) 'Storytelling and the Use of Culturally Appropriate Metaphors in Psychotherapy with Deaf People', in N.S. Glickman & M.A. Harvey (eds), *Culturally Affirmative Psychotherapy with Deaf Persons*. Mahwah, NJ: Lawrence Erlbaum Associates, pp. 169–83.

Fairclough, N. (1992) *Discourse and Social Change*. Cambridge: Polity.

French, S. (1994) *On Equal Terms: Working with Disabled People*. Oxford: Butterworth-Heinemann.

Gergen, K. & Kaye, J. (1992) 'Beyond Narrative in the Negotiation of Therapeutic Meaning', in S. McNamee & K.J. Gergen (eds), *Therapy as Social Construction*. London: Sage, pp. 166–85.

Lenny, J. (1993) 'Do Disabled People Need Counselling?', in J. Swain, V. Finkelstein, S. French & M. Oliver (eds), *Disabling Barriers – Enabling Environments*. London: Sage, in association with the Open University, pp. 233–40.

Marks, D. (2000) *Disability: Controversial Debates and Psycho-social Perspectives*. London: Routledge.

McLeod, J. (1993) *An Introduction to Counselling*. Buckingham: Open University Press.

McLeod, J. (1997) *Narrative and Psychotherapy*. London: Sage.

Oliver, J. (1995) 'Counselling Disabled People: A Counsellor's Perspective'. *Disability & Society*, 10(3), pp. 262–80.

Oliver, M. (1996) *Understanding Disability: From Theory to Practice*. Basingstoke: Macmillan.

Olkin, R. (1999) *What Psychotherapists Should Know about Disability*. New York: The Guilford Press.

Oswin, M. (1990) 'The Grief that Does Not Speak', in D. Dickenson & M. Johnson (eds), *Death, Dying and Bereavement*. London: Sage, in association with the Open University, pp. 296–99.

Ratna, H. (1996) 'Counselling Deaf and Hard of Hearing Clients', in S. Palmer, S. Dainow & P. Milner (eds), *Counselling: The BAC Counselling Reader*. London: Sage, in association with the British Association for Counselling, pp. 234–41.

Reeve, D. (2000) 'Oppression in the Counselling Room.' *Disability & Society*, 15(4), pp. 669–82.

Segal, J. (1989) 'Counselling People with Disabilities/Chronic Illness', in W. Dryden, D. Charles-Edwards & R. Woolfe (eds), *Handbook of Counselling in Britain*. London: Routledge, in association with the British Association for Counselling, pp. 329–46.

Swain, J. (1995) *The Use of Counselling Skills: A Guide for Therapists*. Oxford: Butterworth-Heinemann.

van Deurzen-Smith, E. (1988) *Existential Counselling in Action*. London: Sage.

Withers, S. (1996) 'The Experience of Counselling', in G. Hales (ed.), *Beyond Disability: Towards an Enabling Society*. London: Sage, in association with The Open University, pp. 96–104.

Woolfe, R. & Sugarman, L. (1989) 'Counselling and the Life Cycle', in W. Dryden, D. Charles-Edwards & R. Woolfe (eds), *Handbook of Counselling in Britain*. London: Routledge, pp. 28–42.

4   *Gay Affirmative Practice*

Graham Perlman

The essential ingredient of gay affirmative practice is a therapeutic attitude in which homosexuality is viewed as a viable, constructive way of life compatible with psychological well-being. This attitude can be allied with most counselling and therapeutic approaches used today (see Davies and Neal, 1996, 2000). This may not sound too radical a proposition, however this therapeutic attitude requires rigorous self examination to reach, and constant self-awareness to maintain in the face of an almost overwhelming cultural onslaught against homosexuality.

I will discuss where gay affirmative practice stands today. I will outline the cultural position of homosexuality and the concurrent presence of homophobia and heterosexism in an effort to draw your attention to the internalized beliefs that everyone within the broad cultural influence of the west experiences, regardless of sexual orientation. This discussion will inform our understanding of the potential for harm within the therapeutic encounter, and signpost the journey of self-examination and awareness that anyone wishing to hold the required therapeutic attitude for gay affirmative practice must follow. Finally I will outline some guidelines for gay affirmative practice.

Gay affirmative practice today

Gay affirmative practice is relatively new to the literature in Britain. The ground-breaking series of *Pink Therapy* books (Davies & Neal, 1996, 2000 and Neal and Davies, 2000a) have provided a major contribution to this field locally. Maylon originally described gay affirmative therapy in 1982:

... it represents a special range of psychological knowledge which challenges the traditional view that homosexual desire and fixed homosexual orientations are pathological. ... This approach regards homophobia, as opposed to homosexuality, as a major pathological variable in the development of certain symptomatic conditions among gay men. (1982: 69)

I believe that where gay affirmative practice does happen it is largely by accident or through the efforts of practitioners to apply humanistic value systems thoroughly in their work. Many have encountered lesbian, gay, bisexual and transgender clients in their practice and most would have meant well. However, gay affirmative practice is almost unheard of as a topic within training institutions. Where covered, it is as part of a minor segment of more general discussion on minorities and may require an active request, usually by a gay trainee. (This is based on anecdotal evidence from a wide range of practitioners who were members of the now defunct Association for Lesbian, Gay and Bisexual Psychologies and other contacts.) Gay affirmative efforts will often be made without essential training, formal consideration and effective supervisory and other support.

Gay affirmative practice is not the sole province of the lesbian or gay practitioner. The key element is how individual practitioners, including supervisors, address their own attitudes towards (homo)sexuality. Even people who identify as homosexual may develop behavioural, cognitive and emotional responses which are not affirmative, because of the generalized forces at work.

Homosexuality, homophobia and heterosexism

Homosexuality specifically means sexual desire for people of the same sex, and was long regarded and practised as 'the love that dare not speak its name' (Lord Douglas). In the current writing about gay affirmative practice, consideration of this different sexuality has enabled connection with and/or inclusion of bisexuals and transgender people, and variations in sexual expression within these broad categories. Sexuality is seen to be socially constructed. Gay affirmative practice is likened to 'person affirmative practice' by Neal and Davies (2000b: 1) and many of their contributors assert gay affirmative practice as sexuality affirmative in general.

Homophobia and heterosexism are inextricably linked as psychological processes and cultural phenomena. Homophobia has been variously defined. Davies uses an extended definition provided by Hudson and Ricketts: 'the feelings of anxiety, disgust, aversion, anger, discomfort and fear that some heterosexuals experience around lesbians and gay men' (1996b: 41). For example: a practitioner who wonders how her client can be healthy whilst not desiring a primary monogamous intimate relationship, or shaming looks given by a practitioner when a client talks about fisting. I suggest that the thoughts that support these feelings are an integral part of the psychological system that manifests as homophobia. These feelings and beliefs are generally culturally determined. Each individual will carry their own particular version of that system mediated by their family of origin and own life experiences and decisions. Internalized homophobia is therefore the similar set of feelings and supporting beliefs within someone who identifies as homosexual; for example the discomfort of a lesbian practitioner in discussing her lesbian clients in supervision for fear it might cast shadow on her, or the closeted gay practioner who colludes with his client's notion that it is too dangerous to come out.

Heterosexism is 'the system by which heterosexuality is assumed to be the only acceptable and viable life option' (Blumenfeld and Raymond, 1988: 244). Assumptions of heterosexuality and preconceptions about the nature of the problem when meeting clients of different sexuality are examples of this. It is clearly linked to the system which supports the beliefs and feelings we call homophobia but forms only part of the whole complex of ideas, feelings and actions. Davies (1996b) offers a full discussion of this. I find it easier to see the effects of homophobia and heterosexism and their cultural 'uses' than to explain why they exist at all. I don't propose a definitive explanation for this cultural onslaught, but believe it has to do with the maintenance of power and control, the fear of and fascination with the other and the potential of minority groups placed at the edge of society to cast critical light on that society ... issues of political and psychological resonance which require careful personal consideration by anyone wishing to hold a gay affirmative therapeutic attitude.

The generalised toxic culture

'We [gay people] demand only the freedom to be who we are. The fact that this demand, which takes away nothing from anyone else, is met with such obstinate resistance is a noteworthy indication of how deep-seated is the hostility against us' (Denneny, 1984: 416). This resistance is often bizarre. Non-straight people have been imbued with evil, magic, madness and illness. In Britain conservative agitators have used Section 28 of the Local Government Act 1988, which restricts the use of state funds to 'promote homosexuality' to prevent spending on safer sex campaigns, contributing to the accelerating spread of HIV amongst young people, and the government had to use the Parliament Act to force the equalisation of the age of consent through the House of Lords.

It isn't strange in this context that many activists and others who affirm gayness have come to believe that there must be a reason for this process, that being gay must in itself contain something special that, if not curtailed, controlled and robbed of dignity and justice would provoke wonderful transformation in the world. Unfortunately this is more an attempt to bring meaning to an absurd situation than reality. As a gay man, looking inside myself I see nothing so terribly destructive that requires such censorship over and above that of ordinary society and similarly, although proud of the way in which I have dealt with adversity in my coming out journey, it has not made me any more special than everybody else.

This is a political argument, in the sense that politics has to do with how people experience their selves in the world. This to me is the fundamental business of psychotherapy and counselling. To paraphrase Denneny in 'Gay Politics: Sixteen Propositions' 'Therapeutic endeavour must begin with and remain loyal to our primary experience of ourselves and the world or it degenerates into nonsense, the making of idle theory of which there is no end (and consequently, no seriousness)' (1984: 409). This means the gay affirmative practitioner must seek out any path (for example: literature, art, film, friends, supervisors) which will help them understand the felt experience of their lesbian, gay, bisexual and transgender clients.

There are a myriad of ways in which lesbians and gays experience heterosexism and homophobia. Some are tiny, passing almost unnoticed: a smirk perhaps caught in a stranger's eyes; some everyday: the constant knowledge that laws, attitudes and beliefs view one as shameful; some tragic: like the 'homosexual panic' defence in which 'straight' men are acquitted of murder after describing that their victim had made homosexual advances to them; some acts of omission: when a gay person with a long term partner is invited to the office party alone; and some of commission: where gay people are actively targetted for abuse. Any list would be incomplete.

The culture in which we all grow up is toxic with regard to minority sexualities, as well as other ways of being different, in that it spreads the message 'Don't exist as lesbian/gay/bisexual/transgender' in all the kinds of ways listed above. This wreaks havoc on the souls of those who 'shouldn't' exist and limits the life choices of non-gay people. This message is spread in many self-supporting ways. Lesbians, gay men, bisexuals and transgender people are written out of history and rendered invisible and in turn internalize the necessity to remain invisible. Few positive role models are available in comparison with other minorities. Where visible, we are represented or interpreted as sinful, evil, dangerous, sick or having a shameful secret to be 'admitted'. Violence is unleashed, whether physical or experienced whenever someone makes a comment or 'joke' which robs us of our dignity. This violence is supported by states which implement or enact discriminatory legislation, and the broader cultural representation of homosexuality as shameful.

The erosion of the self begins with the lesbian or gay child's first experience of their sexuality as different. A gay 'census' with 10,500 respondents reveals gay men know of this difference by age 14 on average and lesbians by 16 (*The Pink Paper* 16/11/01). From the moment this person connects with the message not to be lesbian or gay – through that search in the library that only reveals homosexuality and lesbianism associated with bad things, or the shaming look of the person of the same sex who catches an admiring glance, or the bullying or verbal abuse, or even 'harmless' joke that might not even be directed at them but serves as sufficient warning – the lesbian or gay person learns to conceal that part of their identity. In this respect being gay is very different to membership of other oppressed groups like black people and women where 'passing' (acting as if one belongs to the dominant group) is not generally an option. Where passing is possible and consciously or unconsciously chosen as a strategy for survival, it starts to erode everyday relationships. *Every* interaction becomes conditional on the concealment of a fundamental part of the identity.

The felt experience is that 'I can survive only if I deny myself'. This is everywhere, not just in interactions in the sexual arena. 'They like me! What if they knew?'; 'I got the job! What if they knew?' It has a cumulative eroding effect on the developing person's sense of self. I was first consciously aware of my sexual desire for another boy when I was seven. The girl I was sitting next to also fancied the boy so I was immediately aware of her jealousy and intuited that she, and not me, had the right to him. It was a few short steps to being caught looking at an older youth's genitals in the changing room and being shamed, mocked and taunted. I finally acknowledged my homosexuality to myself when I was twenty-two and started to come out to other people slowly after that time. That makes fifteen formative years of felt conditional acceptance and shame about myself.

There is some evidence for a gradual growth in the options available to young lesbians and gay youths. The concerted actions of activists pressing for political change and the general movement for gay people to come out is providing an ever growing support base and making gay people more visible. General media like TV soaps and adverts are gradually representing gay people as 'ordinary', and I think this is having a positive effect for some young lesbians and gays. There is no room for complacency however. Gay people still get bashed and murdered for being gay and governments set the tone, enshrining in law that non-straight people are less than equal. Although extremely difficult to quantify, a British study (Trenchard and Warren, 1984, quoted in Davies, 1996c) has found that at least 20 per cent of lesbian, gay or bisexual youths had attempted suicide and Rivers (2000: 152) found 40 per cent of his respondents in a study on bullying of lesbians, gays and bisexuals had attempted suicide at least once. 50 per cent of gay men and women have suffered a homophobic incident in the last 5 years and 85 per cent of these did not report the incident to the police (*The Pink Paper* 16/11/01).

The counsellor's response

There are two broad ranges of non-affirmative response to lesbian and gay clients: those who want us not to exist; and those who want us not to appear.

Among the counsellors who want us not to exist are fundamentalist religious 'counsellors', and others who claim success in converting people from homosexuality. These people are dangerous in that they deny that the onslaught against homosexuality has any impact on the way homosexuals experience themselves. They are dangerous in that they persist in viewing myths and interpretations of scripture or other works as fact. They are dangerous in that they act as professionals, and therefore powerful members of society, to limit people's life choices. A client of mine observed:

> They offer certainty. I've been seeing you for four years and all I have now is options and possibilities. I feel good about myself, but when I came here I wanted that certainty and I'm sad and pleased it's gone.

The counsellors who want us not to appear are a broader, more subtle group ranging from people who would own that attitude in public to those who wouldn't believe that attitude could be true of them. It includes 'closeted' practitioners, those who think their sexuality is of no importance to the client or their relationship and those who think the client's sexuality makes no difference. Perhaps the most dangerous element of this group are those who mean well, but fail to adequately prepare themselves for the task of providing respect for gay people's lifestyles and life choices. The shaming look consciously or unconsciously manifested in response to their client describing her same sex desire will reinforce the toxic message the client is carrying: 'Don't exist as lesbian', through a demonstration that her therapist will respect her while she talks about other things but not about her (homo)sexuality. This will reinforce the client's sense of conditional acceptance and shame. The client whose sense of self was too fragile at this moment will run and hide, at best carrying with them another confirmation that their sexual nature is unacceptable, or at worst, they would carry out the message. The client with a more robust sense of self might confront her therapist who must be prepared to acknowledge their negative thoughts and feelings. Defensiveness at this moment will only exacerbate the serious harm that could be done. The seriousness is evinced by the fact that this is an existence issue for the (homo)sexual part of the client with suicide a potential worst outcome.

Harmful effects on the healing relationship may be caused by any response which is experienced by the client as confirming their sense that their gayness is shameful. Any intervention which doesn't first offer respect for, and empathic understanding of, how the client felt and what it meant for them may be interpreted by the client as confirmation of their invisibility and consequently be experienced as supporting their shame. For example, simply confronting a client about unsafe sex will be experienced as confirming to the client that their desire is mad/bad/dangerous; that is, shameful. First take the time and trouble to gently ascertain the meaning of unsafe sex for them and what they feel in response to that.

Another danger to the healing process is the failure to understand and explore the impact of heterosexism and homophobia on the client's sense of self. This will be intertwined with the client's other developmental experiences. Some gay children will have had good-enough early relationships and will therefore have a more robust sense of self when faced with the later experiences of knowing themselves to be different and the subsequent erosion of that self. Other gay children will not have received good-enough relating, and therefore manifest the kinds of personality adaptations any child would make in response to their particular early relations. The subsequent effect of conditional acceptance and its erosion of self will then interact with and modify the underlying personality. Sound therapeutic response must deftly unravel both these sets of experiences.

Gay affirmative practice

Gay affirmative practice cannot be simply a cookbook of things to do with gay clients. I believe that is reductionist and contributes to the ongoing perception of lesbian, gay, bisexual and transgender clients as somehow sick, or psychologically maladjusted. It is true that some generalizations can be made. These need to be considered and applied in much the same way as any therapeutic plan deriving from any assessment: with due care and attention to the frame of reference and reality of the client.

I offer here a theory of what gay affirmative practice means that is applicable in all situations. This focuses on the counsellor, not the client, and is an invitation to all practitioners to use the full range of their creativity and responsiveness in their work.

It is our job to engage and nurture the healthy aspects of the client's life force so that they may become fully themselves. What makes this difficult and different with non-straight clients is the power of the generalized destructive messages regarding homosexuality which we all, *regardless of sexuality*, have experienced. This leads to an increased likelihood of destructive transference and countertransference. In other words, when clients exhibit internalized homophobia (the anxiety, disgust, aversion, anger, discomfort or fear of parts of themselves) we are likely to share those feelings about them and ourselves. Unless we have worked through these feelings we will communicate this back to our clients at an unconscious level. Many practitioners, because of the general cultural onslaught against lesbians, gays and bisexuals, will not be aware of elements of that transference, even with supervision, because the cultural imperative will also be shared by those supervisors who have not themselves worked through those feelings.

I use 'working through feelings' as shorthand for developing self-awareness of their beliefs and attitudes about sexuality and difference (which may be masquerading as facts) as well as the feelings they have about them. Also 'attitudes towards sexuality and difference' includes a broad spectrum of beliefs and social systems that extends beyond who one desires and sexual practices, to the way these things are thought about, constructed, organised and regulated by various cultural systems like family, law and the media. A lesbian client noticed that her partner's family treated them with greater respect now they had a baby, perhaps because they seemed more like a 'normal' family.

I believe a conscientious practitioner holding a therapeutic attitude positive towards homosexuality, *provided* they have schooled themselves in the generalized felt experience of being different as our clients experience this, *and* profoundly worked through their responses to the pervasive ideas about (homo)sexuality *before* they start working with clients, is then ready to meet and work affirmatively with the particular experience a gay client presents to them without doing anything else special. See Davies (1996a) for further discussion of this.

I will use some of Denneny's (1984: 409–24) political propositions to highlight the kind of felt experience of the world which arises from heterosexism and homophobia:

Gays insofar as they are gay are ipso facto different from straights.

It is not what we do sexually that is different, rather it is our experience of the way the world views us that makes us different from people whose sexuality is taken for granted. This must be attended to by the therapist despite the distractions of unfamiliar sexual practices or arrangements.

Society does not hate us because we hate ourselves; we hate ourselves because we grew up and live in a society that hates us.

This underlines the importance of understanding lesbian and gay clients from their own perspective and valuing the creative ways they deal with this hatred.

All gays are born into a straight world and socialized to be straight; consequently, we have internalized the enemy, and all political struggle must be simultaneously a self-criticism and self-invention.

This is true of therapeutic endeavour too. Gays must invent themselves and this must be rooted in a thorough understanding of the impact and consequences of internalized homophobia and heterosexism on the self. Practitioners must avoid collusion with this internalized 'straightness'.

The elemental gay emotional experience is the question: 'Am I the only one?' The feeling of being 'different,' and our response to it dominates our inner lives.

The visceral sensation of desire (what one knows with certainty) is intertwined with the devastating possibility that it is dangerous. This traumatizes one's integrity to the point of feeling one's own being is somehow 'wrong'. Empathic understanding is the necessary antidote.

'Only within a framework of a people can a man live as a man without exhausting himself.' (Hannah Arendt)

Few individuals have the integrity or energy to sustain themselves alone. Gay people need to find others who can become their tribe, and practitioners must be alert to this need and support positive attempts to form a gay 'family' or community.

Gay affirmative practice can be incorporated in every area of our work. In the current climate of invisibility it seems appropriate for authors and trainers to specifically outline the relevance or otherwise of their output to lesbians, gays, bisexual and transgender people. Placing equal emphasis on the development of heterosexuality and homosexuality helps avoid the implication of understanding for the purpose of 'cure'.

Conscientious self-examination and the maintenance of an ongoing frame of reference which views homosexuality as a viable option will lead us to identify the everyday experiences that function to maintain heterosexism and homophobia. I believe it is our professional and ethical responsibility to confront these wherever they may harm our clients. Exactly where we draw that boundary is a personal and political choice.

I invite you to enhance your understanding of this by drawing parallels with other culturally stigmatized groups and their generalized sense of self arising from that experience. Some of the processes and responses are similar. The crucial difference with lesbians, gays, bisexuals and transgender people arises through their opportunity to pass as 'straight' and therefore to actually identify with or become the oppressor. This leads to an erosion of the self which is culturally determined.

Gay affirmative practice demands we examine the impact of our culture on both ourselves and our clients. It requires openess to the creativity of stigmatized people's responses to their world. Understanding the ways in which many 'things' such as sexuality, relationship patterns and the family are pervasively experienced as being fixed, whilst we know they are socially constructed, offers the opportunity to free our clients from self-hatred and rigidity so they can be fully themselves.

Further Guidelines for Gay Affirmative Practice

Many authors have done this before. See, in particular Kowszun, 2000.

- Being gay affirmative means developing awareness about the *current* cultural climate and implies choosing how to intervene in this.
- With all issues a client brings ask yourself how this might have been shaped by their gayness and the world's response to that.
- Wonder about the way sexuality/family/gender are constructed by the cultures we live in. Looking at history will bring the peculiarities of the present into focus.
- Don't buy into the idea that gay is better or worse than anything else.
- Inform yourself by any reliable means possible about the wide range of ways lesbian, gay, bisexual and transgender people live their lives

today. Exploring gay history will demonstrate the creativity and changes in style and content.

- Familiarize yourself with all the sexual possibilities and language so that you won't be shocked or suprised just by their mention.
- Imagine a world where a fundamental part of your identity required hiding. What would help you to value yourself in such a world?
- Support any creative efforts by your gay clients to connect with other gay people in satisfying ways.
- Remember that even very young people have nascent sexual identities.
- Take good account of the fear of gay people about revealing their sexual orientation. The dangers are real, as are the possibilities for living openly.
- Acknowledge any homophobic and/or heterosexist thoughts and feelings you bring into the encounter. Similarly help your client to identify those they bring.
- If you can't move that part of you that would rather gay people weren't seen, refer your lesbian and gay clients on and work on it with your own support system rather than them.

References

Blumenfeld, W.J. and Raymond, D. (1988) *Looking at Gay and Lesbian Life*. Boston: Beacon Press.

Davies, D. (1996a) 'Towards a Model of Gay Affirmative Therapy', in D. Davies and C. Neal (eds), *Pink Therapy: A guide for counsellors and therapists working with lesbian, gay and bisexual clients*. Buckingham: Open University Press, pp. 24–40.

Davies, D. (1996b) 'Homophobia and Heterosexism', in D. Davies and C. Neal (eds), *Pink Therapy: A guide for counsellors and therapists working with lesbian, gay and bisexual clients*. Buckingham: Open University Press, pp. 41–65.

Davies, D. (1996c) 'Working with Young People', in D. Davies and C. Neal (eds), *Pink Therapy: A guide for counsellors and therapists working with lesbian, gay and bisexual clients*. Buckingham: Open University Press, pp. 131–48.

Davies, D. and Neal, C. (eds) (1996) *Pink Therapy: A guide for counsellors and therapists working with lesbian, gay and bisexual clients*. Buckingham: Open University Press.

Davies, D. and Neal, C. (eds) (2000) *Therapeutic Persectives on Working with Lesbian, Gay and Bisexual Clients*. Buckingham: Open University Press.

Denneny, M. (1984) 'Gay Politics: Sixteen Propositions', in M. Denneny, C. Ortleb and T. Steele (eds), *The View From Christopher Street*. London: Chatto & Windus – The Hogarth Press, pp. 409–24.

Kowzun, G. (2000) 'Gay and Lesbian Affirmative Therapy', in C. Feltham and I. Horton (eds), *Handbook of Counselling and Psychotherapy*. London: Sage, pp. 628–33.

Maylon, A. (1982) 'Psychotherapeutic Implications of Internalized Homophobia in Gay Men', in J. Gonsiorek (ed.), *Homosexuality and Psychotherapy*. New York: Haworth Press.

Neal, C. and Davies, D. (eds) (2000a) *Issues in Therapy with Lesbian, Gay, Bisexual and Transgender Clients*. Buckingham: Open University Press.

Neal, C. and Davies, D. (2000b) 'Introduction', in C. Neal and D. Davies (eds), *Issues in Therapy with Lesbian, Gay, Bisexual and Transgender Clients*. Buckingham: Open University Press, pp. 1–6.

The Pink Paper. London: Chronos Publishing Services.

Rivers, I. (2000) 'Long-term Consequences of Bullying', in C. Neal and D. Davies (eds), *Issues in Therapy with Lesbian, Gay, Bisexual and Transgender Clients*. Buckingham: Open University Press, pp. 146–59.

5 Woman Centred Practice – Two Perspectives

(i) Jocelyn Chaplin – The rhythm model

No woman is an island. We are all deeply entangled in the complex web of the social, economic and cultural worlds in which we live. When an individual woman comes for counselling she brings her 'social unconscious' as well as her personal one. She brings her language and models of how the world is structured, as well as the particular words spoken in the sessions. These ideas are all formed in a world that is still basically patriarchal, where the models that underlie everything are still largely hierarchical (Chaplin, 1998). Everything is divided in our minds into opposites: masculine/feminine; public/private; objective/subjective; outcome/process. One side is deemed superior and must win and/or rule over the other. Opposites that are typically associated with women, for example subjective, private, vulnerable etc., are devalued, thus maintaining women's oppression. At this underlying, structural level the female, feminine and women are still thought of as inferior in most parts of the world.

There has been a massive, but subtle backlash against feminism. Glossy magazines for men hide rampant sexism with 'sophisticated' articles. The pornography industry has gone from being worth £30 million in 1986 to £60 billion today (*Observer*, 21/01/01). Many men today at least pay lip service to equality, but often unconsciously feel that they are *supposed* to be superior. The rage that some men can experience at women's growing power is expressed in increasing violence against women. Since 1981 the largest increase in violent crimes has been in incidents of domestic violence (British Crime Survey 1996, Home Office).

Many women come for counselling because of such violence, but many more come because they are suffering from patriarchy's hierarchies in less obvious ways. Assertion deficits, low self-esteem, depression – and verbal and emotional abuse can be deeply damaging, even when it is not physical. The mode of win/lose thinking destroys thousands of relationships, including those between same-sex couples.

Sexualities are also still deeply distorted by patriarchal attitudes, despite all the information now available. In some ways women are trying so hard to fit in with male requirements, that they are not fully exploring their own, often different sexuality. Shrof talks of women's relationship with sex and food: 'Appetites for food and sex are hence also socially regulated and patriarchal societies tend to characterize women's appetites as dangerous, and to act as suppressants of them' (1993: 11). Millions of women hate their bodies. Increasingly young girls are starving themselves to fit with those 'taunting' figures in the magazines. I would not always work with a woman in helping her to 'lose weight'. This could be colluding with the social pressures that make her obsessed with slimming. I would ask her what it means in terms of her own bad feelings about herself or about her 'fat' side. I would help her explore those social pressures and to get in touch with her own needs. However, we do need to acknowledge, as suggested by Hutchinson, that as women we 'have built our identities around the struggle between ourselves and our bodies. Letting go of negative body attitudes threatens the very foundation of how we see and construct our lives' (1994: 165).

While expectations of women have rocketed over the past thirty years the reality for many, perhaps most, has been as difficult as ever. What is sometimes called equality feminism (Greer, 1999) has not necessarily brought with it the real equality in which women's values are respected as much as males'. Women have simply adapted very successfully to the masculine modes of thinking and behaviour. Even in the world of counselling, that can be thought of as a 'feminine' skill, male structures are increasingly taking over. The emphasis on measurement, making lists and testing is an example of the encroaching masculinization of counselling.

Either/or, hierarchical thinking is the underlying structure for much of our psychological misery. Many difficulties that women bring to counselling are vital survival mechanisms in an 'unhealthy' society. Baker-Miller reminds us that women's very strengths such as caring and nurturing are labelled weaknesses in patriarchal society. We also need to address other hierarchies such as 'race', class, disabilities and sexualities by exposing the ways in which 'hierarchalizing difference, can lead to the lower side being turned into an 'other', and being defined by the higher opposite' (1978: 31–51). Often clients will hierarchalize different sides of themselves so much so that they do not recognize these unacceptable sides of themselves at first and when they do, they are seen as inferior. Therefore, in deconstructing the ways in which hierarchical thinking impacts upon the psyche we need a model that both recognizes and dissolves 'inner hierarchies'. In considering the masculinization of counselling, we need to avoid falling into the trap of either/or thinking, and instead of masculine and feminine skills competing against each other we need to model them in 'rhythm' together.

The rhythm model

A rhythmic approach to understanding change, growth and life, provides a way in which counsellors can actively seek to address the hidden hierarchies that serve to maintain women's oppression. It moves away from pro-hierarchy to pro-equality. In contrast to a 'control' model, a rhythm model is the dance between one opposite side and another. It does not propose that change and life is a climb towards the peak, the success, or the goal. Instead it can be seen as ongoing movement, a dance and even a struggle arising from the tensions between opposites. Counselling becomes, therefore, a rhythmic process of separating, understanding and accepting the opposites. It enables us to live life as a rhythmic dance between and within the opposites.

Stages to being in rhythm

- Building trust – the 'mothering' phase
- Identifying themes – separating out the opposites
- Exploring the past – understanding the opposites and inner hierarchies
- Dissolving the inner hierarchies and facing ambivalence – accepting the opposites
- Making changes – living with the opposites.

Building trust – the 'mothering' phase
I use the term mothering in the symbolic sense to represent containment and unconditional acceptance. Mothering has become devalued in male patriarchal society, resulting in millions of 'unmothered' children. Many have internalized the higher valuing of mind over body and taken on the patriarchal fear of, as well as fascination with female bodies. A woman coming for counselling then may need to get back in touch with her

natural body, to rediscover her bodily feelings. This requires the counsellor to play the role of accepting mother, comfortable in her or his own body, solid and present.

Identifying themes — separating out the opposites

After establishing a therapeutic alliance and building trust we begin to uncover the hidden hierarchies by identifying patterns and themes in the client's behaviour and thinking. For example 'Laura' had 'hierarchalized her different sides so much that she only really identified with that of the career business manager. The identity associated with mothering was not even recognized at first. And even when she did recognize this side it was seen as very inferior. She also saw them as either/or choices in life…'

Exploring the past — understanding the opposites and inner hierarchies

In exploring a client's past it soon becomes clear which of a pair of opposites she was placed in as a child. 'I was the bright one', or 'the pretty one' or 'the good one' or 'the naughty one'. Often lurking beneath the main opposite is the feared 'other side'. Labelling children 'clever' or 'stupid' can be damaging either way. Children internalize the opposites in the same extreme divided form. It is not recognized that these are false opposites expressed within a framework of hierarchical thinking. In reality everyone is both clever and stupid in different aspects of their lives at different times. A woman who feels that she must always be the best, or be perfect, may have a fear that if she isn't, she is a total failure. Modern society does not foster the ability to appreciate and accept all the opposite sides of the same person. It cannot accept the different ways in which everyone is clever and stupid, succeeding and failing.

Dissolving the inner hierarchies and accepting ambivalence — accepting the opposites

Having gained some understanding of the main themes and inner hierarchies in which we have rejected parts of ourselves, the next task is to learn to accept those rejected opposite parts. We need to accept our vulnerability as well as our strength, our anger as well as our gentle side. For a lifetime clients have experienced these opposites within them in a hierarchical way, one side on top and the other inferior. One is good; the other is bad. We have felt that the 'strong' side must control the 'weak'. Instead of seeing the different sides of ourselves as hierarchical, I use the 'ancient model of constant rhythmic change between opposites. A client who is depressed because the sad side of life has not been accepted can learn to accept the rhythm of life between happiness (outgoing energy) and sadness (in-going energy).' This part of the process is where the client begins to learn to cope with the reality of ambivalence. It may be the time when the client begins to see people, including the therapist, as both good and bad, accepting and rejecting, strong and weak. Accepting and even enjoying the fact that things can be both one thing *and* another. 'To live rhythmically is to live with uncertainty, undecidedness, forever open, in process and unfinished' Chaplin (1988, 1998).

Making changes – living with the opposites
This stage of the process is a time of loss as well as gain, losing the belief that one is always 'nice' or a 'victim', accepting the other side too, and so losing the illusion of one-sidedness. With this comes the possibility of shedding our childhood dreams. We need dreams however as well as reality for the process of growth. It is not necessary to *stop* dreaming, rather to know what are our dreams and what are our realities. As women our realities have been socially constructed, i.e. we have been socialised to take care of others and suppress our own needs in the service of other people. In this stage a woman can become easier with both sides of her nature, experiencing her rhythms of anger and love consciously, rather than thinking she must always be nice. She can learn how to accept *and* reject people and situations. It is important for a woman to learn to reject and criticize, particularly if she has been accepting of everyone and everything. Another aspect of women's socialization is to be nurturing and giving. Learning to live with the rhythmically interconnected opposites of giving *and* receiving can be difficult for women.

Conclusion

As counsellors we need to be aware of any ways in which we might reinforce the hierarchical relationships many women have within the patriarchal world. We need to be aware of the conflicting opposites that dominate women's psyches, for example the desire for intimacy and fear of rejection; being totally in control or in complete chaos; dependence and independence; power and powerlessness; perfection and uselessness. We need to move towards psychological androgyny (Singer, 1976). We all have abilities and characteristics associated with the masculine and the feminine. To allow these abilities to emerge gives us greater opportunities to dance more freely the lives that we were born for.

As counsellors we also need to develop an awareness of our own inner hierarchies, and explore how they impact upon our own lives and our work with clients. There are hierarchies everywhere. For example, when asked to contribute to another academic text on feminism and psychotherapy I found myself strangely full of fear. As I explored this within myself I realized the fear was of a superior authority. It was the kind of fear that hierarchies create. I was afraid 'superior' academic feminists might attack me for being too essentialist, not feminist enough, as if my kind of feminism would be seen as 'inferior'. In writing this chapter I offer a feminist perspective that encourages women to reclaim and embrace those parts of us that may otherwise have been lost. It also provides an alternative model of counselling, thinking and being in the world, that goes to the deep structural roots of discrimination.

References

Baker-Miller, J. (1978) *Toward a New Psychology of Women*. Harmondsworth: Penguin.

Chaplin, J. (1988) *Feminist Counselling in Action*. London: Sage.

Chaplin, J. (1998) 'The Rhythm Model', in I. Bruna Seu, & M. Colleen Heenan (eds), *Feminism and Psychotherapy – Reflections on Contemporary Theories and Practices*. London: Sage, pp. 135–56.

Greer, G. (1999) *The Whole Woman*. London: Doubleday.

Home Office (1996) *British Crime Survey*. London: HMSO.

Hutchinson, M.G. (1994) 'Imagining Ourselves Whole: A Feminist Approach to Treating Body Image Disorders', in P. Fallon, M. Katzman & F. Wooley (eds), *Feminist Perspectives on Eating Disorders*. London: Guildford Press, pp. 152–68.

Observer Magazine, 21, January 2001.

Shrof, F.M. (1993) 'Deliciosa, the Body, Passion and Pleasure', in C. Brown, & K. Jasper (eds) *Consuming Passions – Feminist Approaches to Weight Preoccupation and Eating Disorders*. Toronto: Second Story Press.

Singer, J. (1976) *Androgyny*. New York: Doubleday.

5 *Woman Centred Practice — Two Perspectives*

(ii) Bonnie Burstow — A radical feminist therapy perspective

I am inviting readers to consider a radical perspective on working with women. Significantly, the *immediate context* in which this manuscript is written is a book called *Radical Feminist Therapy* (Burstow, 1992), in which I attempted to delineate emancipatory practice with women clients. The *larger context* is the reality of ongoing oppression. Radical feminist therapy has its origins in three movements — radical therapy, radical feminism, and antipsychiatry. The premises of radical therapy are best summed up by Hogie Wyckoff's (1980: 15–16) famous formula:

Oppression + Lies + Isolation = Alienation
Action + Awareness + Contact $\longrightarrow$ Power

The implication for counselling which follows from this formula is that counselling is benign and effective only to the extent that it counters lies, challenges oppressions, fosters connection between people similarly oppressed and culminates in action. The second perspective — radical feminism — includes an analysis of the feminization of poverty while focusing on the reduction of women to a body, which is for men. As counsellors that work with women, it is vital that we take in the degree of that reduction and of that violence. It is not simply a matter of understanding that an alarmingly high percentage of our female clients are raped. Counsellors need to understand that:

- Women are systematically reduced to a body for the sexual gratification of men and for the menial serving of men even where no overt violation occurs.
- In peace and war, the patriarchy wrests control of their bodies away from women.
- Compulsory motherhood and romantic love are part of women's bondage.
- All women live with *covert* violation and under the threat of *overt* violation, whether it be sexual violation or battery.
- Woman as body is inferiorized, afforded less money, freedom, and credibility.
- Women's problems in living largely arise from and are exacerbated by the intersections of sexism and other systemic oppressions.

Taking seriously the third of these movements – antipsychiatry – means challenging the patriarchal conceptualizations of 'normal' and working at unhousing the psychiatrist within. As shown in works such as Burstow (1992), Chesler (1972), and Lewis (1999), throughout its history, psychiatry has pathologized women's ways of thinking and acting insofar as they differ from men's and/or are not in men's gender interests. Correspondingly, it has locked women up in institutions and further violated women with 'treatments' like electroshock. Feminist therapy has long been committed to problematizing psychiatry. A radical feminist therapy orientation goes further. It calls on counsellors to avoid diagnosis altogether, not to use the psychiatric system, to help women protect themselves from this patriarchal and otherwise hegemonic system, and to validate even those ways of coping and thinking that may initially seem 'crazy'.

Alongside these commitments, a radical feminist therapy approach necessarily involves addressing women in their diversity. A woman-centred approach which takes the white middle class, able-bodied, heterosexual woman as the norm is not simply inadequate; it is harmful. By way of example, counsellors who automatically assume that their women clients grew up with the message not to be strong minimally create cognitive dissonance with a high percentage of their black clients and working class clients. However much they may try to be 'open minded' or 'tolerant', counsellors who have not worked on their own lesbophobia inevitably convey the message that lesbian relationships either are not acceptable or are second best.

Overall view of the work

As with all feminist approaches, though to a greater extent than others, a radical feminist therapy orientation emphasizes the significance of power, beginning with the power differential within the therapy relationship. As Burstow (1992) and Greenspan (1983) point out, it is critical not to duplicate the huge power imbalances of patriarchal psychiatry. We diminish the power differential by sharing our interpretations, by not forcing our own agendas on our clients, and by negotiating goals and processes in good faith.

It is important to attend to the individual woman's specific social location and jeopardy. We attend properly to location by being aware of race, ethnicity, age, class, sexuality, ability, religion, and other aspects of our client's situation and taking responsibility to respond with these in mind. We attend to oppressions specifically by asking ourselves how our clients are oppressed and how concretely these oppressions play out in our clients' lives.

Examples of questions we might ask ourselves in situations of difference are:

- Is it safe for this woman to talk about being raped during the war or will divulging the rape cause her to be ostracized by her community? (see Cole et al., 1992).
- What are the multiple forms of drudgery imposed on this black working class client? How does it feel cleaning white women's homes as well as her own?
- How is society likely to respond to disabled women actively engaging in heterosexual sex? To disabled women engaged in lesbian sex?

The prevalence of violence against women requires that radical counsellors working with women be particularly attentive to issues of violence. In this regard, questions which we might ask ourselves when seeing a new woman client include:

- Is this woman very thin? If so, she may be ill. Alternatively she may have an eating problem; and childhood sexual abuse may be implicated.
- Is this woman bruised? If so, potentially, she is being battered.
- Does this woman avert her eyes when I look at her? If so, cultural differences are a possibility. So is current or past abuse.

With a radical orientation, an additional layer is added to empathy. The counsellor is called upon to engage in *political* empathy – that is, empathy based on recognition of the woman's political plight. An example of political empathy from a recent session is:

> *Client:* I'm upset. I couldn't see my mom because I couldn't afford the plane fare. I'm sick to death of having to watch pennies all the time.
> *Burstow:* I'm so sorry. I know how much you were looking forward to seeing her. And of course having to watch your expenses so closely year after year wears you down. Women's wages in this society are an absolute obscenity; and who wouldn't be sick to death?

Empowering work with women necessarily involves helping our clients counter internalized oppression – oppressive views of themselves, oppressive views of all women or all women similarly situated. One viable way to proceed, at least initially, is mutually uncovering and co-investigating scripts that may be interfering with the client's life. Sexist scripts are a particularly important area for co-investigation. A sexist script is a sexist blueprint which a woman received early in life, telling her how to think of herself and act – a blueprint that she is still following, perhaps out of awareness. Examples of typical sexist scripts are 'Super-mom' and 'Just a Good Fuck'.

Given how depressing oppression is and given the mainstream injunction against women getting angry, not surprisingly, women tend to get depressed. On an emotional level, our job as counsellors is often to invite anger. On a cognitive level, it is to depathologize and politicize the depression. It is to help women to see the commonality between their situation and the situation of depressed women similarly situated and to locate the fundamental problem in social structures – not in themselves.

A radical feminist therapy orientation, additionally, involves helping women reclaim control of their bodies – saying 'no', deciding on their own body weight, getting back in touch with what feels right and good. And, insofar as possible, it moves toward contact and action. Examples of empowering types of contact are: getting together with other child-hood sexual abuse survivors, joining a women's consciousness-raising group, and joining a woman of colour collective. Examples of empowering acts are: leaving the batterer and taking part in the annual 'Take Back the Night' march.

There are a number of issues that come up repeatedly in work with women, including childhood sexual abuse, eating problems, adult rape, depression, and battery. It is critical that counsellors educate themselves about all of them and be able to work with all in empowering ways. I will provide more detailed radical commentary on the first two.

Childhood sexual abuse

Brown (1995) estimates that one in every three women has been sexually abused by the time she reaches sixteen. Burstow (1992) and Lobel (1986) suggest that childhood sexual abuse be conceptualized as a continuum on which all women are located, for all women grow up under a patriarchy which sexualizes little girls. The *covert* sexual violation inherent in everyday sexism severely alienates women from their bodies. *Overt* sexual violation – especially overt childhood sexual abuse – compounds the injury. Trusted others – generally people who were supposed to protect the child – undermined her very being-in-the-world. As shown in Herman (1992) and Burstow (1992), the result is ongoing traumatization, generally characterized by repression, enormous sensitivity to triggers, fragmentation, numbing, and various other modes of coping that work and backfire at the same time.

Radical work involves taking the violation very seriously wherever it may be on the continuum. It means believing women. It means helping women move beyond denial, self-blame, and minimizing; it means respecting women's ways of coping and working toward a better mutual understanding of them – whether these ways be dissociation, self-injury, or eating problems. It means helping the women create more safety and integration *without expecting that the trauma can be 'cured' or thinking that the women either can or should move toward regarding the world as an essentially safe place.* Despite the theorizing of feminists like Herman (1992), note, as Lewis (1999) suggests, given a sexist society where the triggers are always there and which *really is* unsafe for women, such expectations and goals are ultimately liberal and unaware.

The most serious mistakes that a counsellor can make when dealing with childhood sexual abuse is not believing the client or holding the client responsible. Insofar as the counsellor doubts the client, the client's worst fear is confirmed – that nobody will believe her. Insofar as the counsellor holds the child in any way responsible, the counsellor exacerbates the internalized oppression. Other costly errors include: retraumatizing the client by not building in safety measures such as going at a slow pace; not understanding the significance of particular women's ways of coping such as self-injury and therefore trying to stop the client from using them; and forcing mainstream understandings and solutions on women from non-dominant cultures.

An incident from my own practice illustrates the significance of respecting women's coping skills. I was supervising counsellors running a group for incest survivors. A member of the group turned up one day badly injured and badly shaken. She had cut herself but had no awareness of doing so. I suspected that cutting outside of awareness was a solution to an impossible position in which someone had put her. On investigating further, we discovered that the client routinely cut as a way of distracting herself from the pain of childhood abuse and that her therapist had forbidden her to cut. Not able to cut in awareness, as doing so meant risking her therapeutic relationship, and needing to cut, the woman now cut out of awareness and in the process injured herself far more than usual and profoundly frightened herself. The solution, which was quickly put into practice, was to join with the client on the validity of cutting, advocate on the client's behalf to have the injunction against cutting removed, honour the coping, and explore its meaning. To the best of my knowledge, the woman never again cut outside awareness.

Eating problems

It is important to recognize that eating problems, like childhood sexual abuse, are endemic to women, although there are clear cultural differences. It is helpful to conceptualize it as a continuum also, ranging from traditional 'dieting' to advanced anorexic and bulimic solutions. It is critical, correspondingly, to see that society is implicated in women's eating problems. As writers like Orbach (1988) illustrated long ago, dominant cultures have promulgated sexist beauty ideals based on self-deprivation, becoming weightless/worthless. Women are socialized to feed others and to deprive themselves. Correspondingly, as women are reduced to body and as women have little control in the real world, it is natural that women turn to controlling their own bodies. Indeed, troubled eating is best understood as a solution to the problems of being a woman in a sexist society – including the problem of childhood sexual abuse. The anorexic solution, for instance, can be a way of getting rid of a woman's body and so a way for the childhood sexual abuse survivor to avoid sexual triggers. And the bulimic purging may be a triggered response to oral sexual abuse.

As Orbach (1988) has documented, conventional practice with eating problems involves individualizing, pathologizing, blaming, and attempting to control women's food intake; and as such, as Burstow (1992) suggests, it perpetuates the sexist assault on woman as body and turns the counsellor into an enemy. A radical orientation begins with rejecting this approach, politicizing the woman's plight, and respecting women's right to do whatever they wish with their own bodies. More detailed work includes:

- De-emphasizing the issue of food.
- Validating and honouring the coping.
- Co-investigating the different meanings which the coping holds.
- Helping the client deal with underlying issues.
- Helping women make very gradual changes in their eating patterns if and *only if* they wish to.
- Co-exploring alternative or auxiliary means of coping – other forms of resistance and other forms of control in particular.
- Helping the woman exercise more power in the larger oppressive world.

Closing Remark

I have suggested a radical frame for working with women clients. And throughout, I have highlighted problems inherent in conservative and liberal frames. In closing, I would refer readers to my book, Burstow (1992), for more detailed information. And I would invite counsellors to work on their own attitudes and to radicalize their approach. I would also draw attention to the importance of combating sexism and other systemic oppressions *outside* as well as *inside* counselling. As Whalen (1996) suggests, as we counsellors restrict anti-oppression work to the counselling session or even to the larger engagement with clients *per se*, we fall into liberalism.

References

Brown, L. (1995) 'Not outside the normal range', in C. Caruth (ed.), *Trauma: Explorations in Memory*. Baltimore, MD: The Johns Hopkins University Press.

Burstow, B. (1992) *Radical Feminist Therapy*. Newbury Park, CA: Sage.

Cole, E., Espin, O. & Rothblum, E. (eds) (1992) *Refugee Women and their Mental Health*. London: Harrington.

Chesler, P. (1972) *Women and Madness*. New York: Doubleday.

Greenspan, M. (1983) *A New Approach to Working with Women*. New York: McGraw Hill.

Herman, J. (1992) *Trauma and Recovery*. New York: Basic Books.

Lewis, T. (1999) *Living Beside*. Toronto: McGilligan Books.

Lobel, K. (ed.) (1986) *Naming the Violence*. Seattle, WA: Seal Press.

Orbach, S. (1988) *Hunger Strike*. New York: Avon.

Whalen, M. (1996) *Counseling to End Violence Against Women*. Thousand Oaks, CA: Sage.

Wykoff, H. (1980) *Solving Problems Together*. New York: Grove.

6   *Child-centred Counselling Practice*

Barbara Smith and Mark Widdowson

We were all meant to shine as children do

Marianne Williamson

Counselling is slowly becoming part of the mainstream response to children presenting with distress and 'challenging behaviour'. In this chapter we explore some of what children and young people need from us as therapists, from other adults and from the wider society in which they are socialized. We consider ways of supporting black, disabled and working class children, and young gays and lesbians, in a profession largely populated by white, middle class, enabled therapists.

It is a constant source of amazement to us that given the histories some children bring to therapy, they still choose to put their faith in another adult. With the privilege of working with children comes a responsibility on the part of counsellors/therapists to take seriously the needs and rights of children and to advocate on their behalf in a society which says that hitting children is legal (and helpful) as long as you don't leave a bruise. What is termed 'smacking' children is considered 'assault' in the adult world. There is an irony in the notion of an ever developing and highly sophisticated government-led child protection system, operating in parallel with a refusal by that same government to outlaw the physical punishment of children within their families. A report by Save The Children (2001) highlights physical punishment of children as a global problem, documenting some worrying statistics; in Korea a survey found that 97 per cent of children had been physically punished, many severely; in Kuwait a 1996 survey of parents' attitudes found that over half agreed or strongly agreed with severe beatings 'in cases of gross misbehaviour' and 9 per cent of parents agreed with burning as a form of punishment; in the UK, government-commissioned research showed three quarters of a large sample of mothers admitted to 'smacking' their baby before the age of one. In families where both parents were interviewed, over a third of children were hit weekly or more often by either or both parents, and a fifth had been hit with an implement. Is it any wonder then that one in five children in Britain are considered to have a mental health problem? Article 19 of The UN Convention on the Rights of the Child states clearly 'All appropriate legislative, administrative, social and educational measures to protect the child from all forms of physical or mental violence, injury or abuse, neglect or negligent treatment, maltreatment or exploitation, including sexual abuse, while in the care of parent(s), legal guardian(s) or any other person who has the care of the child...' The Committee on the Rights of the Child has this to say – 'The legal and social acceptance of corporal punishment of children, whether in their homes or institutions, is not compatible with the Convention' (2001: 7). They recommend campaigning to raise awareness of the negative effects of corporal punishment and to encourage the development of positive, non-violent childrearing and educational practices. We would recommend that anyone working with children's health and happiness at heart align themselves to such campaigns.

Which children and what do they need?

Hirst suggests that 'one in five children has some form of mental health problem, ranging from eating and attention deficit disorders to conditions such as depression' (1999: 19). Other issues children and young people bring to us are the pain of parental separation and divorce, family violence, bereavement, separation anxiety, and low self-esteem. We also encounter children suffering from racial, sexist and homophobic bullying from peers. Children referred from the Local Authority care system have often had multiple traumas such as sexual and physical abuse, and always the devastation of separation and loss. Children who are asylum seekers or refugees will often have suffered deep trauma, separation, loss and bereavement, as well as the persecution they often endure in their 'refuge'.

Despite the concerns we express in the previous section, there does on another level seem to be a sense that as a society we are beginning to take children's emotional health seriously. At the time of writing government funding to the tune of £84 million has been put aside for early years initiatives such as Sure Start and parenting programmes, aimed at giving under 4s the best possible start, and the Children's Fund supports projects for 5–13 year olds. CAMHS (Child and Adolescent Mental Health Services) teams are operating nationwide, and the free helpline CALM (Campaign Against Living Miserably), aimed at reducing the suicide rate amongst young men, is well underway. School counselling is also on the increase and emotional literacy is now on the agenda for school age children. School mentors and circle time are some of the ways in which schools are responding to the ever increasing difficulties that children are dealing with in the current age.

Who's the therapy for?

Government funded programmes are often concentrated on those children and young people who are displaying the very worst in distressing and challenging behaviour – behaviour which distresses and challenges adults. This can often result in 'quick fix' strategies such as anger management, which may be a poor substitute for exploring the underlying distress that a young person's 'acting out' symbolizes. Children will act out what they can't talk out and we practise caution in how we respond to those young people who are 'troubled and troublesome'. It may be that what *this* child needs is an opportunity to *express* anger in healthy and constructive ways.

Parents and other adults often refer children in the hope that the therapy will create changes *they* want in the child – to 'sort the child out' in terms of their behaviour. This can be at odds with what the child is expressing – the child may need a space to express their troubles and concerns with a caring and understanding ally. We consider 'acting out' behaviours to be coping mechanisms – a defence against distressing feelings, and that these defences should be honoured as survival strategies. Docker-Drysdale gives an example of her work with a young woman:

> The mother of a patient said to me recently. 'Jane is quite unmanageable. We had a terrible day – she has ruined our family life with her violence'. When I asked in some detail about this day in Jane's life, I found that she had been persecuted, frustrated and deprived by her parents and the rest of her family. Furthermore, her mother told me about a series of episodes which all reflected very badly on herself and Jane's family, without noticing that this was so, that Jane's reactions were the inevitable result of intolerable stress. (1990: 126)

Experience has taught us that if we take care of the heart and underlying pain, the behaviour will follow.

Contracting

English (1975) refers to this three-way dynamic of child, parent(s) and therapist as requiring a 'three handed contract'. We believe it is important to have these different 'agendas' out in the open and that each talks honestly about what the different parties are seeking from the work. Many of the children that we work with are being looked after by the Local Authority. By definition they will often have had the experience of sudden loss, over which they had no control. They go on to 'act out' their distress in substitute families, and subsequently the new carers ask for them to be removed, usually at short notice and always reinforcing the child's self image as bad, unmanageable, unlovable etc. This can happen numerous times in a short space of time (some children having had as many as eight placements in a year) culminating in a fear of any kind of attachment relationship to defend against the terrible pain of loss and rejection. Barbara Smith makes it clear to referring adults that the child should have some control over the ending of the therapy. It is better not to enter into a therapeutic relationship at all than to reinforce history with the sudden ending of an important relationship, over which the child has no control. Steiner suggests 'Guardians will, for one reason or another, decide to discontinue therapy – particularly if the child begins to exhibit some changes after a period of therapy. Frequently this decision is based on their notion that their child is getting worse, instead of better' (1974: 249).

Communication with referring adults and children

Clear communication and co-operative relationships with significant adults is crucial for effective therapy with children. We have found parents to be open to direct advice and honesty about how they can support their child's therapy. One child came for therapy to increase her confidence and self esteem. It transpired that she was being bullied emotionally and physically by an older sibling, which was largely ignored by her parents. It was explained to her parents that any successful work in therapy sessions is undermined when a child does not feel safe even in their own home. We need to be potent in our discussions with parents, modelling being a child's 'protector'. However, this requires skilled communication so that parents do not feel threatened by the relationship between child and therapist. This is counter-productive and unhelpful for children – blood is thicker than therapy!

As we know, communicating with children is largely similar to that with adult clients but requiring some additional skills, knowledge and abilities. We need to have a sense of humour and fun at the same time as taking their problems and hurts very seriously indeed. Mark Widdowson describes his first meeting with a fifteen year old who was clearly very uncomfortable about seeing him. She sat with her arms crossed, a scowl on her face and speaking to him in monosyllables, then saying 'Well, have you got any advice for me then?' 'Yes I have' he said, 'Use moisturizer every day.' She scowled, paused and broke into laughter – 'You're mad you.' She never missed an appointment in six months. Other children of course are so terribly anxious and afraid that they require a very gentle, respectful approach, speaking quietly and 'waiting lovingly at the boundary' (Little, 1999).

We have found it helpful to have lots of creative media – paints, clay, puppets, books and musical instruments to express feelings through play. Play is to children what language is to (most) adults. They will express their troubles through play in ways that may symbolically re-enact conflict and express needs.

Risk and resilience

A document published by the Department for Education and Employment (DfEE) 'Promoting Children's Mental Health within Early Years and School Settings' (2001) highlights a number of factors that have an impact on children's mental health. They identify certain groups who are more at risk of developing mental health problems than others, those risks being located in: the child; the family and the community. They also identify factors that increase resilience in children and promote children's future mental health (see Figure 6.1).

Given the knowledge we have of the experiences of black, disabled and working class children, it is clear from this framework that they are at a distinct disadvantage. For example, three risk factors in the community that leap out (at least to us) are those of socio-economic disadvantage, homelessness, and discrimination; while a high standard of living and good housing are identified as resilience factors in a child's life. We want to consider ways in which we as therapists can support these children in our work both within the therapeutic relationship and outside the therapy room.

Black children

Black children face racism on a daily basis. We are not just referring here to racist bullying by individuals, either through verbal or physical abuse.

Risk Factors	**Resilience Factors**
In The Child ❑ Specific learning difficulties ❑ Communication difficulties ❑ Specific developmental delay ❑ Genetic influence ❑ Difficult temperament ❑ Physical illness especially if chronic and/or neurological ❑ Academic failure ❑ Low self-esteem	**In The Child** ❑ Secure early relationships ❑ Being female ❑ Higher intelligence ❑ Easy temperament when an infant ❑ Positive attitude, problem-solving approach ❑ Good communication skills ❑ Planner, belief in control ❑ Humour ❑ Religious faith ❑ Capacity to reflect
In The Family ❑ Overt parental conflict ❑ Family breakdown ❑ Inconsistent or unclear discipline ❑ Hostile or rejecting relationships ❑ Failure to adapt to a child's changing needs ❑ Physical, sexual or emotional abuse ❑ Parental psychiatric illness ❑ Parental criminality, alcoholism or personality disorder ❑ Death or loss – including friendships	**In The Family** ❑ At least one good parent-child relationship ❑ Affection ❑ Clear, firm consistent discipline ❑ Support for education ❑ Supportive long-term relationship/absence of severe discord
In The Community ❑ Socio-economic disadvantage ❑ Homelessness ❑ Disaster ❑ Discrimination ❑ Other significant life events	**In The Community** ❑ Wider supportive network ❑ Good housing ❑ High standard of living ❑ High morale school with positive policies for behaviour, attitudes and anti-bullying ❑ Schools with strong academic and non-academic opportunities ❑ Range of positive sport/leisure activities

Figure 6.1   *What Causes Mental Health Problems in Children and Young People? DfEE (2001)*

We are talking about institutional racism; that which leaves black children unprotected or harassed by police, teachers having low educational expectations of black children and a media which does not reflect the multicultural society in which they live. How then, do we as therapists approach these problems, which can rock a child's self esteem and leave them vulnerable to difficulties in developing a healthy black identity? Banks suggests:

> Children from minority ethnic groups have specific identity needs related to knowledge about origins of self, of culture and identity, which may require considered and systematic input if the child is to develop psychological completeness. To ignore this need is to ignore a fundamental developmental need of a child, with the effect of disadvantaging the child in later life in its understanding and degree of comfort with self. (2001: 142)

Black children need a positive racial identity and this can be supported by therapists affirming their 'blackness'. It is their physicality that singles them out for racism and it is important therefore to allow their physical beauty to be celebrated.

Good practice indicates that ideally a therapist would have the same 'racial' background as a child they are working with in terms of providing a positive role model. Children need to be able to talk about their experiences of racism and this is where a black worker can offer an empathic ear. They can also learn from a black therapist how to develop strategies for dealing with racism and be praised for their coping skills. However, when working cross-culturally, the therapist should have access to a same 'race' supervisor or consultant. Play materials should be culturally appropriate and reflect a multi-racial society in work with *any* child. We have found it helpful to create a 'life book'. This is similar to life story work undertaken with children who have had multiple carers and are living separately from their birth families. The life book however is an opportunity for children to bring photographs of themselves in various situations, for example, hobbies, day trips, birthdays etc. and to talk about themselves in those situations. This gives the therapist opportunities to give positive affirmations while looking at the photographs, to affirm the child's black identity. 'Look at your lovely warm smile on this one', affirming their physicality, or 'You look like you're concentrating really hard on that puzzle', affirming their intelligence. The book cover is usually a work of art and children often want to do some of the artwork or writing at home.

Work undertaken in the therapy room with a child can be undermined by their experiences at school where racist bullying can be rife (particularly in a school where most of the children and staff are white). School head teachers have been known to respond to racist bullying by saying 'There is no racism in this school' and 'Children have to find their place in the world and to learn to stick up for themselves'. We see this as a failure to protect children from emotional abuse and that it amounts to neglect. We are mindful that bullying features highly in statistics of young suicides and attempted suicides. An *anti-oppressive* approach is one which challenges oppression, and to this end we would suggest that it is our duty as therapists to intervene if necessary and to advocate on a child's behalf if they are being racially bullied in any way. Lines cites Payne's approach to bullying:

> the practice of giving victims strategies for social survival fails in recognizing the true culprits of bullying behaviour. He believes that the work should be focused upon the bullies rather than their victims (who merely need support) and that school systems ought continually to confront bullying head on, since the common practice of school bullying is a reflection of unchallenged societal attitudes of abusive power and exploitation. (2002: 104)

Young people's sexuality

What *are* we teaching our children about sexuality? 'Gay' is currently a fashionable term of abuse between children in the playground and serves as a powerful warning to young people to consider heterosexuality as an only option. This puts young people who begin to experience attraction to same sex partners at severe risk of psychological distress.

There has been a marked aversion on the part of those who have responsibility for the care of young people to affirm their sexuality as lesbians, gays and bisexuals (LGB), largely due to a fear of being on the receiving end of disciplinary measures. The now infamous Section 28 of the Local Government Act 1988 has been cited as a direct cause of reluctance in supporting young LGB people, and in tackling homophobic bullying. Recent debates on the issue of Section 28 and the reduction and equalizing of the age of consent have invariably included an element of 'protecting young people from sexual predators'. The evidence, however, suggests that the opposite is true. Denying young people information and support places them *more at risk* in so far as they are not equipped to protect themselves. Our experience of working with young LGBs has taught us that the necessity of secrecy of same-sex sexual activity prevents them from gaining adequate protection. When legislation leads to such oppression of young LGBs , it is our stance, as *responsible* adults, that we would not deny young people such protective information and support, even if required to do so by a court of law.

Young gay people often have a much harder time than their heterosexual counterparts. Results of a study by D'Augelli et al. (2001) found that nearly half of LGB youth interviewed had contemplated suicide and a third had made at least one suicide attempt. Around a third of the respondents in this study clearly cited their homo/bisexuality as the primary cause of their suicidal thoughts and behaviour.

Given the degree of vulnerability of young LGB people to verbal and physical abuse, the process of disclosure (coming out) should be handled sensitively and with care. Young people, once adjusted to their sexuality are inclined to want to tell lots of people. Many of those people will be affirming and supportive. However, as therapists, it is important to help the young person, without being alarmist, to assess the possible hostile consequences of disclosure, such as rejection and violence, and to help them to develop a supportive network. It is helpful to avail ourselves of information regarding local LGB youth groups (in all major cities and towns) and even consider taking the young person to such a meeting. As LGB young people have been socialized as heterosexuals, and given the osmotic absorption of norms and ways of operating in heterosexual relationships which are not relevant to these young people, alignment with positive role models and alternative support networks is crucial in developing positive self-esteem.

There is speculation about whether a LGB therapist may be more appropriate for a young person exploring their sexual identity. However, we believe the single most important factor is that the young person feels safe with a therapist who offers an affirmative response in seeing their sexuality in a positive light and in guiding them towards, or providing them with information through literature, films and magazines, which affirm their sexuality, so that they may take up their place as equal citizens. It is essential that we consistently acknowledge *homophobia* as the 'problem', *not* their homosexuality nor homosexual desires.

Working with disabled children

If we return to the risk and resilience framework in predicting children's mental health (Fig. 6.1.), we will see that perhaps the most significant risk factors within the child lie within those children who are physically or learning disabled. Disabled children have traditionally been overprotected and their skills, intelligence and abilities discounted. Finkelstein and Stuart suggest:

> All too often both professionals and parents unthinkingly collaborate in pro-
> tecting disabled children from risk-taking and personal responsibility. A conse-
> quence is that disabled children can grow into adulthood poorly equipped with
> the social skills necessary to form meaningful relationships, to compete for
> jobs and to sustain their own independent households. (1996: 178)

They argue that disabled children are often prevented from developing into active, confident and knowledgeable citizens, through the denial of opportunities for learning the same social skills as 'non-disabled' children.

The provision of 'special' schools for children with 'special needs' is a contentious issue for many of those with the needs of disabled children at heart. Finkelstein and Stuart refer to segregated schooling as a 'devastating consequence' of the welfare mentality hailing from a 'conspiracy of protection' between legislators, service providers and carers. They offer suggestions for inclusive education where:

> good quality access, small class size, well-trained support workers and personal assistance can all contribute to the move away from a problem oriented approach which pays too much attention to what disabled children cannot do rather than the disabling barriers which may prevent success in achieving the goals which they have set for themselves. (1996: 180)

As therapists we can draw from these insights so that we do not reproduce this overprotective stance in our work with children, and discount the *abilities* of disabled children. The consequences of overprotection of children can result in feelings of helplessness, powerlessness and identity problems. (Of course there is also the danger of 'under protection' in that they may be more vulnerable to abuse by adults due to limited verbal communication and relative isolation.) For whatever reason the disabled child enters counselling, we should be mindful of the fact that such children have often been socialized to be dependent and as such may have internalized the view that they cannot achieve or do things for themselves. It is for this reason that we employ a 'strengths model' focusing on what the child *can* do, and away from what the child cannot do due to impairment. A creative and innovative therapist will undertake social skills work and increase assertion, helping to strengthen a child's self image. For some children it may be helpful to use a multi-sensory approach and relaxation and music can play a great part in this.

Clearly, poor access is disabling for children who use wheelchairs and our place of work should be accessible to *all* children. It would also be advisable to familiarize ourselves with the progressive Coalitions of Disabled People for advice and information.

A brief word on children and class

The 'risk and resilience' framework in Figure 6.1. gives a clear indication of the vulnerability of working class children to mental health problems. Issues relating to class are often overlooked in discussions of anti-discriminatory or anti-oppressive practice and this class-blindness can have huge implications for working class children. Children are very aware of class difference and a 'posh', middle class therapist may not get past 'first base' with some young people. If we, as therapists take a position of valuing more highly 'middle class' culture and norms, then we fall into the trap of non-acceptance and may attempt to teach children middle class values. We need to work to understand the social world of the child within her or his own cultural context.

Most of our learning about these issues comes from the children and young people themselves. Barbara Smith recalls a session with a sixteen-year-old young woman, Katie, who was in the care of the Local Authority and who was seeking to get fit and find interesting things to do with her weekends. The therapist told her about walking and youth hostels, explaining that groups of walkers often stayed in the hostels when they had been walking in the daytime. One of her carers telephoned to clarify what the therapist had been suggesting, saying that Katie was showing an interest in the idea, but that she had explained to the carer 'you go to a hostel with other homeless people and you all walk round together in the day'. The therapist had completely missed her worldview. The only association she made with hostels was of hers and her family's experience of homelessness and walking was certainly not done in hills. The irony for the therapist was that she, as a working class woman, would not have had experience of hill walking or youth hostelling at sixteen either!

Summary and suggestions for good practice

As counsellors, much of our work is picking up the pieces of what could be avoided by creating a culture where love and protection of children are viewed as a birthright. We offer the following as a bottom line in working with children and young people.

- Be aware of current child care policy and child protection procedures.
- Support initiatives which impact positively on the lives of young people.
- Be aware that children who are 'different' will be acutely aware of their difference and need affirmation *for* that difference.
- Be congruent (they'll know).
- Check out community resources which support young LGB, black and disabled children and young people.
- Be aware of a young person's history: they may have had multiple placements; themes of loss and rejection figure highly in young people's troubles.

- Be willing to enter the young person's frame of reference, see the world as they see it and move gently, respectfully and potently within this frame of reference.
- Be willing to act as an advocate for children and young people.
- State the obvious when others can't see the wood for the trees.

References

Banks, N. (2001) 'Assessing Children and Families who belong to Minority Ethnic Groups', in J. Howarth (ed.), *The Child's World – Assessing Children in Need*. London: Jessica Kingsley Publishers.

D'Augelli, A.R., Hershberger, S.L. & Pilkington, N.W. (2001) 'Suicidality, Patterns and Sexual Orientation-related Factors among Lesbian, Gay and Bisexual Youths'. *Suicide and Life-Threatening Behavior*, 31: pp. 250–65.

DfEE (2001) *Promoting Children's Mental Health within Early Years and School Settings*. Nottingham: DfEE Publications.

Docker-Drysdale, B. (1990) 'The Management of Violence', in *The Provision of Primary Experience*. London: Free Association Books.

English, (1975) 'The Three-cornered Contract'. *Transactional Analysis Journal*, 5(4), pp. 383–4.

Finkelstein, V. & Stuart, O. (1996) 'New Services', in G. Hales (ed.), *Beyond Disability*. London: Sage.

Hirst, J. (1999) 'Growing Strong', in *Community Care*. 13–19 May, pp. 18–19.

Lines D. (2002) *Brief Counselling in Schools – Working with Young People from 11–18*. London: Sage.

Little, R. (1999) *Workshop Presentation Notes*. Canterbury: ITA Conference.

Save the Children (2001) *Ending Corporal Punishment of Children – Making it Happen*. London: Save the Children.

Steiner C. (1974) *Scripts People Live*. New York: Grove Press.

Submission to the Committee on the Rights of the Child. (2001) *General Discussion on Violence against Children within Family and Schools*. Ohio: Centre for Effective Discipline.

7 *Counselling Older Adults*

Ann Orbach

The word 'ageist' defines the particular bias that allows '… those of us who are younger to see old people as 'different'. We subtly cease to identify with them as human beings, which enables us to feel more comfortable about our neglect and dislike of them … Ageism is a thinly disguised attempt to avoid the personal reality of human ageing and death.' (Butler, 1975: 893).

The word ageism is comparatively new, but the prejudice has earlier roots and seems to be a phenomenon of our western culture with its emphasis on a person's usefulness and productivity. According to Freud, '… near or above the fifties the elasticity of mental process on which the treatment depends, is as a rule lacking … old people are no longer educable' (1905: 264). As for women: 'Her libido has taken up final positions … there are no paths for future development; it is as though … indeed the difficult development to femininity had exhausted the possibilities of the person concerned' (1933: 169).

When is 'older' and what does it look like?

One of the assumptions in ageism is the habit of lumping older people together as 'the elderly' – irrespective of race, class, sexuality or gender. This arbitrary grouping covers a span of two generations between early 60s and 90s – at least 30 years. We need to remember that people do not necessarily age according to years lived. Each person's pace is individual.

Old age as 'disease'

Ageism views growing old as a downhill process. There is an expectation of arthritis, heart failure and unstoppable decline, mental as well as physical. Old people's pain, physical and emotional, tends to be treated with palliative drugs and anti-depressants rather than (the more expensive) counselling.

Research by Age Concern uncovered evidence of age discrimination at all levels of the NHS (Gilchrist, 1999). A Gallup Survey in 1999 showed that one in twenty people over 65 had been refused treatment, while one in ten had been treated differently after 50. This included 40 per cent of coronary care units attaching age restrictions to the use of clot-busting drug therapy, the refusal of kidney dialysis or transplants to 66 per cent of patients aged 70–79, and no invitations to breast screening for women of 65 and over. There was also an inappropriate use of anti-psychotic drugs in care homes. Despite government assurances of equal treatment, the evidence from patients and their relatives showed that, in many cases, hospitals were failing to provide essential care. Although many patients in the survey spoke up when invited to, others suffered in silence. 'Many people of my generation see doctors as Gods and would never contradict them' (Bennet & Cass, 1998: 3). Older adults come to feel that they are expendable. While young people are viewed as having something to contribute to society, older people can see themselves as a burden and a drain on resources, leading to internalized ageism.

Many misleading myths about ageing bodies and minds need exploring. Far from being rigid in their attitudes (as Freud maintained), older people have proved themselves remarkably adaptable in a century of unprecedented scientific and social change. Research provides evidence that, given a normal level of physical health and mental activity, there is *no* inevitable decline in cognition. On the contrary, there are indications that, in most individuals, intelligence may actually increase even in their 80s (Jarvik, 1991). The adult brain is now seen as capable of structural modification as a result of psychological stimulation *and continuing use.* Thus modern research attests to the complexity of the body/mind interface and promises much potential for growth and change in the second half of life (Nemiroff & Colarusso, 1985: 17–18).

The value placed on youth

When these older people were young, they were taught to respect their elders. They may have anticipated that one day they would have earned some of that respect themselves. Young people are valued for their energy and new ideas. 'Dominant ideology sees the future, and the people of the future, as crucially important, and older people have little role there' (Scrutton, 1999: 17). The media reinforces youth's importance. Outward appearance is what counts. Society's consumers, while still young and wrinkle-free, are offered a whole range of products to postpone the 'horrors' of advancing age.

The dominant image of older people is one of dependency, which 'takes away the adult status and personhood of the elderly [*sic*] ... The bodily betrayals of old age can therefore result in a stigmatizing process which has been referred to as the "mask of ageing", pointing to the inability of the body to adequately represent the inner self' (Featherstone & Wernick, 1985: 7).

Institutional ageism

Individuals working with older people may have consciously worked to overcome their own prejudices but are likely to be affected by those of the organizations for which they work. In homes for older adults, whether NHS or private, dependency is too often taken for granted, and efforts on the part of residents to hold on to their self-respect are seen as stubborn or 'naughty'. A counsellor, visiting a 76 year-old in hospital, found her sessions constantly interrupted; in spite of the 'DO NOT DISTURB' notice on the door.

> M commented that her time with me was the only time when she was allowed any privacy. She explained how she had been left sitting on the toilet with the door open while the nurses chatted outside ... she expressed feelings of despair at her loss of dignity and independence. (Brotherton, 1995)

In a long-stay geriatric hospital, staff have been observed protecting themselves unconsciously from close contact with ageing and death. They often need counselling, just as much as the residents, if they are to cope constructively with their anxiety (Terry, 1997).

It seems that the best way to combat institutional ageism may be the growth of counselling services that are specifically geared to treat older people. In those that already exist, it is hoped that careful choice of counsellors, ongoing training, supervision and personal therapy, will decrease prejudice and foster a better understanding of age-related problems.

Internalized ageism

It is hardly surprising that neglect and disrespect in older age often produce the knock-on effect of old people ceasing to believe in their own worth. This internalized bias against him/herself may find fertile ground in a person's inner world, already shaped by the rules of a strictly disciplined upbringing. Older women have not been encouraged enough to assert themselves, while men have moulded their characters to accord with social expectations of 'manliness', to keep a stiff upper lip and never give in to weakness. When expectations fall away and society sees only failing strength, disempowerment is likely to follow. If referred for counselling, such clients may find it difficult to get started. They may be apologetic about their neediness and hesitant in talking about intimate matters, perhaps for the first time.

> A civil servant was reaching the peak of his career when faced with the rule of enforced retirement at 60. At 59 he had been valued. A year later, he was only fit, he said bitterly, for the scrap heap. Soon after giving up work he developed various ailments and had a minor operation. 'So they were right', he said, 'I'm past it'. His work had been all-important. Without it, he felt that he had lost his identity. He showed all the symptoms generally associated with bereavement. His counsellor had to do more than empathize. She worked on widening his horizons to embrace new choices that he had, up until now, been too single-minded to entertain. Together, they explored his early life and how, before embarking on a successful career, he had been bullied by a stern father, who taught him to scorn any kind of failure. In fact, he never failed but the push towards achievement had taken its toll. His body was telling him to relax. It took him a long time to recover his self-worth and to realize just how many doors could still open for him.

This client had lived with ageism all his life and absorbed ageist attitudes. Some people have no built-in mechanisms against discrimination. Their own ageing creeps up on them surreptitiously. They do not feel different, nor do they feel old, unless jerked into a sudden realization that society perceives them as in the old age category. They have no pride in age and no defence against it (Scrutton, 1999).

Attachment or disengagement?

Bowlby (1980) describes attachment behaviour as seeking to maintain strong affectional bonds. If there is no secure base in childhood, fear and anxiety may persist throughout life, affecting adult relationships and future experience of loss. Disengagement theory (Cummings and Henry, 1961) sees ageing as a gradual process of separating individuals from their social roles and interests. According to this theory, the process is natural and is also positive insofar as separation results in reflection and self-sufficiency. In contrast, Havighurst (1969) maintains that individuals prefer to remain active and involved with other people. Both extremes – involvement or withdrawal – fail to take account of individual differences or the influence of early experience. Disengagement feeds too conveniently into ageist attitudes to be accepted without question. Having to retire at a fixed age, expectations of ill health, failing intellect, giving younger people opportunities – are all pressures on older adults to stand aside.

On the other hand, Havinghurst's Activity Theory (1969), with its opposite expectations, risks intruding on those who want time to be alone, quietly reminiscing and attempting (with or without counselling) to find meaning in their lives. Reminiscence therapy, along with introspection, has in the past been considered potentially unhealthy, but it is currently gaining acceptance as helpful therapy.

Some disengagement may become essential but that does not mean it is easy to let go of familiar roles.

> A client of 80 sought counselling because of an itching skin. Her only son had divorced his first wife, the mother of her grandchildren, whom she had got to know and love. He produced a new daughter-in-law, about whom the older woman had nothing good to say. She stifled her anger but produced a fiery rash. The doctor found nothing wrong and told the counsellor that her need was psychological. What soon emerged was her pain at having lost her 'mothering' role. When her son first married, he and his wife had both been very young and grateful for the 'mothering' she gave them. Now she felt pushed aside. She had lost her son to another woman. As she got older, she complained that no one in the family informed her about what was going on, her opinions were not asked and no respect given to her age and experience. The counsellor gently pointed out that she was not respecting her son as an adult but still treating him as a little boy. She had to get older still, frail and nearly blind in order to realize how much both her son and his second wife cared for her welfare and were prepared to look after her. All her life, she had nursed other people. Needing to be needed was her way of being in control, and it was hard to be the recipient of other people's care. Yet she could gratefully accept any caring that came from the counsellor, who was her secure base. The skin rash cleared up, as no longer needed, once she had faced her anger at being displaced, and allowed herself to recognize her daughter-in-law as a caring person.

Older adults and sex

If old people are sexually active or have erotic fantasies, young people would rather not know. Despite the 'permissive' society, there seems to be one taboo that persists – sex is only for the young. For those who were children before World War II, the subject was shrouded in secrecy. There was no sex education at school, and parents, if persuaded to mention it at all, tended to become embarrassed. Masturbation caused shame and the threat of madness. There was an assumption that girls should be virgins when they married but that boys might benefit from some prenuptial experience, though this bit of sexual inequality was unlikely to be referred to openly.

For these children, who have now grown old, life seems to have come full circle. Yesterday's unenlightened children find themselves treated as though they had never had any sex. But their much more knowing sons and daughters, schooled in Freudian theory and the Oedipus complex, find themselves uncomfortable with the idea of their parents as sexual beings, a discomfort which extends to all old people, so that the general assumption seems to be that women lose interest after the menopause and men either become impotent or have to boost their sagging virility by pursuing younger women. Sex among older people, if acceptable at all, must be turned into a joke.

A difficulty in counselling older clients, who have been strictly brought up, is their view of sex as indecent and the shame attached to still wanting it. Counsellors can help break down barriers of reticence and shame, but opening up the subject is never easy. Counsellors need to face the prejudices of society and, more important still, their own discomforts. We need to tread carefully, remembering the heavy taboos that used to hamper communication and often inhibited sexual intimacy among couples. Sadly, the problem is more likely to be a lack of partners (especially for women) than lack of desire, and there may be considerable mourning for lost lovers.

The situation is well summed up by a Jungian analyst: 'An old person who loses his partner is not less lonely than a young one, but his loneliness has little remedy; one can scarcely start being promiscuous in old age, but many recent studies have shown that sexuality knows no age limit, and it is cultural prejudice that makes old people give up their sex life … our culture has not changed much in its prejudices against the elderly who still seek physical and spiritual love, and we have no concern for their sexuality which offends our aesthetic taste' (Zoja, 1983: 55).

Multiple oppressions

If merely being old creates oppression, how much greater is the potential discrimination and oppression of being 'old' and black, 'old' and gay or 'old' and disabled?

Black and minority ethnic clients

Counsellors need to be aware of the difficulties that these clients may experience in looking for counselling in what may seem to be an alien culture. Some would argue that only counsellors who share a similar background would be able to work with black elders, though as this country becomes increasingly multi-cultural and the profession begins to address racism, we may hope to see some of the barriers coming down. There are many subtle ways in which unconscious racism may affect our attitudes. As counsellors, we need to avoid 'lumping' non-white groups together as 'black elders' and ignoring the specific histories and cultural identities of West Indian, African, Chinese and Asian people. Alibhai-Brown quotes an older black woman: 'You don't need books girl. We are all different and all God's children. Don't go around putting us together like a basket of oranges now. I won't have it' (1998: 81).

A 1998 survey by Age Concern showed many gaps in support programmes for older people in the setting up of counselling services. This was particularly marked in the lack of provision for black and Asian elders. Very little information was forthcoming, but interviews in two centres revealed a general lack of mental health care for these groups, who all too often face isolation and invisibility (Bennet & Cass, 1998). At SubCo Elders Day Centre in Newham, East London, the Asian community has set up its own centre. Opening in 1993, help has been enlisted from Age Concern, Social Services, the Housing Department and Health Authority. Among other projects, the Shanti Counselling Service has been running, with varying degrees of success, since 1997 'for Asian Elders wanting emotional support and wanting to share their experience in a safe place' (Annual Report, SubCo Shanti Counselling Service, 1999). Problems highlighted have been loneliness, difficulty in adjusting to a new culture and the westernised attitudes of children and grandchildren.

Older gays, lesbians and bisexuals

The Age Concern report states 'Older men believe that you only get counselling if you are "sick" and a bit weird, whilst younger men see it as a more natural activity. This is exacerbated in a rural area where there is a greater sense of isolation and lack of visibility of the gay community, and thus a fear of being "found out"' (Bennet & Cass, 1998: 19).

Counsellors working with older gay men, or older lesbians, should be mindful of how hidden and shameful their sexuality used to be in the time of their youth when 'coming out' was unthinkable and perhaps more dangerous than today. This modern phenomenon of 'coming out' has been described as a 'developmental process' (Zera, 1992), in which case the older gay person will have missed out on an important rite of passage. For men, one needs to remember that homosexuality, even between consenting adults, was a punishable offence. For women, there was no law to condemn them but conventions and parental disappointment got in the way of openness and they often found themselves living a lie, unable to conform to society's expectations. Acceptance by an affirming counsellor will be helpful in mourning losses which may never have been acknowledged – youthful looks, unborn children and the deaths of partners, unrecognized by their relatives and friends. By understanding both sides of the family equation, a counsellor may help in easing bitterness and bringing about reconciliation with the discriminations and disappointments of the past.

Disabilities

Young and non-disabled people are inclined to expect disability in their elders and are surprised when it is absent. Would-be helpers often get pushed away if too eager to take an old person's arm in anticipation of a fall, instead of asking first if the arm is wanted. It can be hard to stand and watch determined efforts at independence, without intruding our more 'effective' younger selves. Stirling suggests 'A valued life would allow the experience of risk and stress, and would not solely aim to exclude or minimize discomforts ... The achievement of a risk-free state of contentment may be the common view of the goals of later life but it is a view always reserved for others ... For "us" the hurly-burly of life in real time, places and activities is of the highest value' (1996: 407).

Deafness in older people is a frequent disability, but often provokes only impatience in younger people. 'Why can't Mum get herself a hearing aid?'. People are likely to be more patient with blind people and their more obvious need of help. Loss of memory can also be irritating, but is a very real concern for the person to whom it happens. An 80-year-old woman asked her counsellor if she had noticed her memory getting worse. She wanted an honest answer and was relieved, rather than depressed, when this was recognized. The only reassurance the counsellor could give was that the total loss we call dementia would not necessarily result. In many cases, people have coped with disabilities all their lives, but, when they grow old, these get discounted and assumed to be just a normal part of ageing, rather than a separate issue. Counsellors need to be alert to the distinction, as another example of the assumption that old age is, in itself, a disease.

Dementia

The onset is usually gradual. It is important that counsellors and carers do not write off what is being said by people in their confusion. Often, there is meaning in the confused talk, which takes on a metaphoric quality and may be possible to interpret in the same way as a client's dreams. Body language also conveys meanings, which can be helpful in communicating feelings and thoughts in the therapeutic process.

Class and poverty

In the world of psychoanalysis, psychotherapy, and to some extent counselling, practitioners tend to be white, middle-class and well educated. On the whole, the clients referred to them have the same background, and that is especially true in private practice, though it is hoped that those who also work in NHS clinics may drop elitist assumptions and realize that the treatment on offer should depend neither on social class nor age.

Retirement, which is a socially created milestone, almost unknown before the 20th century, may have a liberating effect on 'pensioners' who can afford a good life-style, but for those who have to rely on the state pension, there can be basic worries about the necessities of life; food, clothing and keeping warm, with little money for a social life and luxuries. 'It has been calculated that over two million people live close to or below the official poverty line ... The growing proportion of elderly people within the population is frequently cited by the media as a burden upon tax payers' (Scrutton, 1999: 32).

Age affirmative practice

How can counsellors develop a positive approach to ageing and older clients? 'Old age brings with it problems few of us have faced up to, often because it is more comfortable for us to deny them; they might after all happen to us one day' (Scrutton, 1999: 8). It goes without saying that those undertaking counselling with people much older than themselves need to look into their own futures and imagine what the process of ageing will be like, the inevitable losses and also, some gains. They need also to face, and be able to think about their own deaths. No doubt this is a daunting task but essential in reminding us that 'the elderly' are not a separate species. We too are ageing. *'They'* are *us*.

Counsellors need a sense of history, so that they can see some of the background to the stories their clients tell them. Only by paying attention to what was going on around older people 'back then', socially, politically, economically, can the counsellor get some idea of how much the problems presented have to do with the historical context of these people's lives and how much belongs to individual human development.

Theories of development, from Freud onward, place far more emphasis on infancy than on adult life. Few would seriously dispute the importance of early experience in, for instance, establishing Bowlby's (1980) 'secure base' or Winnicott's (1975) 'good enough mothering' without which insecurity persists. Erikson's eight stages of ontogenesis expand the Freudian model. Each stage needs successful negotiation before moving on, the last task of all being to arrive at integration in the face of despair. In his later years, Erikson posited a ninth stage and a more fluid interpretation of his earlier stance, suggesting that people move on but also revisit their earlier conflicts. Nothing is solved once and for all, and there is no inevitable despair. What emerges is 'Wisdom – a kind of detached concern with life itself, in the face of death itself, as expressed both in the sayings of the ages and in those simplest experiences which convey the probability of an ultimate meaning' (Erikson, 1981).

By listening carefully to our clients' stories – and old people are the traditional story tellers – the counsellor can help people to dwell on successes and joys, even in the midst of loss, so that there is always something to celebrate as well as much to mourn. Part of a counsellor's affirmation will be helping the client to let go of ego-centred desires and become aware of valued parts of the self that can be passed on to future generations.

There is much political activity by older people putting themselves in the forefront of social change. The recent government initiatives under the heading 'Better Government for Older People', are giving older people a voice in improving public services as well as combating age discrimination. The International Year of Older Persons, 1999, set out to improve media images, especially those depicting older people as victims. In America, the Gray Panthers movement has managed to stop enforced retirement at 65, exposed elder abuse in nursing homes and campaigned for better health care. Together, they empower each other, and in the words of their founder Maggie Kuhn:

> Speak your mind – even if your voice shakes.
> Well-aimed slingshots can topple giants.

Finally, I would like to cite some late-life successes: Copernicus was 70 when he published his first and last book and founded modern astronomy. At 70, Golda Meir became prime minister of Israel. And at 77, Gandhi won independence for India (Orbach, 1996: 8).

Some suggestions for anti-discriminatory practice when working with older people

- Old age is not a disease needing diagnosis and cure, but a stage of development with problems to be addressed and worked through.
- Counsellors need to challenge ageist assumptions, both in society and in themselves, in order to empower their older clients.
- Older people often have to relinquish some of their earlier roles, as sexual beings, parents and workers, to mourn their losses and find a balance between attachment and disengagement. They may need help in coming to terms with their position in the life cycle and encouragement in exploring whatever new experiences are still open to them.
- Older people need to be listened to as they strive to find meaning in their life stories, accept the reality of death as a final letting go, and trust that they are bequeathing something of value to a new generation.
- Acknowledge and appreciate the wisdom older people have to offer.

References

Alibhai-Brown, Y. (1998) *Caring for Ethnic Minority Elders, A Guide*. London: Age Concern.

Bennet, A. & Cass, C. (1998) *Counselling Work with Older People, A Report on Behalf of Age Concern*. England's Activ/Age Unit.

Bowlby, J. (1980) *Attachment and Loss: Loss, Sadness and Depression*. London: Hogarth Press.

Brotherton, C. (1995) *Social and Legal Context of Counselling*. West Sussex Institute of Higher Education (Diploma in Independent Professional Counselling).

Butler, R.N. (1975) 'The Elderly: An Overview.' *American Journal of Psychiatry*, 132, pp. 893–900.

Cummings, E. & Henry, W.E. (1961) *Growing Old, The Process of Disengagement*. New York: Basic Books.

Erikson, E. (1965) *Childhood and Society*. Harmondsworth: Penguin.

Erikson, E. (1981) 'Elements of a Psychodynamic Theory of Social Development,' quoted by P. Hildebrand, 'Object Loss and Development in the Second Half of Life,' in *The Race Against Time*, Nemiroff & Colarusso (eds) (1985) New York: Plenum. Press.

Featherstone, M. & Wernick, A. (1985) *Images of Ageing: Cultural Representations of Later Life*. London and New York: Routledge.

Freud, S. (1905) *On Psychotherapy, S.E. vii*. London: Hogarth Press.

Freud, S. (1933) 'On Femininity', from *New Introductory Lectures*. Harmondsworth: Penguin.

Gilchrist, C. (1999) *Turning your Back on Us: Older People in the NHS*. London: Age Concern.

Havighurst, R.J. (1969) 'Research and Development Goals in Social Gerontology, Gerontology Society Committee on Research,' *Gerontologist*, 9 (4).

Jarvik, L.F. (ed.) (1991) *Comprehensive Review of Geriatric Psychiatry*. London: American Psychiatric Press.

Nemiroff, A. & Colarusso, A. (1985) 'Adult Development: A New Development in Psychodynamic Practice', quoted in *The Race Against Time*. New York: Plenum Press.

Orbach, A. (1996) *Not Too Late: Psychotherapy and Ageing*. London: Jessica Kingsley.

Scrutton, S. (1999) *Counselling Older People: A Creative Response to Ageing*. London: Age Concern.

Stirling, E. (1996) 'Social Role Valorisation: Making a Difference to the Lives of Older People?', *Handbook of Clinical Psychology of Ageing*, Woods, R.T. (ed.) Chichester: Wiley.

Terry, P. (1997) *Counselling Older People and their Carers*. London: Macmillan.

Winnicott, D.W. (1975) (first published in 1945) 'Primitive Emotional Development' in *Through Paediatrics to Psychoanalysis*. London: Hogarth Press, pp. 145–56.

Zera, D. (1992) 'Coming of Age in a Heterosexist World: The Development of Gay and Lesbian Adolescents', *Adolescence*, 27, pp. 849–54.

Zoja, L. (1983) 'Working Against Dorian Gray: Analysis and the Old', *Journal of Analytical Psychology*, 28, pp. 51–64.

8 Counselling and Religion

Nick J. Banks

Freud is often seen as the father of counselling in that he initiated its early practice or 'caused' practice as a reaction against his views. Freud attempted to apply psychoanalysis to religion in his early writings. His view (1921) was that all religion is a religion of love only for those who embrace it. On the other hand, for those who do not belong to a pre-scribed religion, cruelty and intolerance are encountered. Freud's belief was that this, with every religious faith, was a natural way of behaving to outsiders. Jacobs (1992) contends that Freud saw religion as a universal obsessional neurosis on one hand and individual neurosis as a private religion on the other.

This chapter will explore the importance of examining a counsellor's attitudes and prejudices in relation to people whose religious beliefs differ from their own. It is important to acknowledge that it is argued there is a difference between 'religion' and what others may term 'spirituality'. Pederson suggests that, whereas spirituality tends to be more inclusively defined as 'one's place in the universe, religion refers to the specific religious faith and practice resulting from a person's spirituality. Spirituality is broader and more inclusive in meaning than religion.' (1997: 100). Spirituality may have to do with humanism and not necessarily have a formal or defined religious connection. Thus religion tends to refer to specific faiths and practices whereas spirituality tends to describe the more broad and inclusive phenomenon. Religions tend to involve moral systems. These influence and in some cases regulate and determine the behaviour and social perceptions of a group and individuals within the group by the laying down of values of what is considered right and wrong. Jacobs argues that Freud saw the function of religion as giving people information about their origins and the beginnings of existence. Thus it had a function creating and maintaining identity. Its goal was to assure them of protection and of ultimate happiness in the 'ups and downs' of life. Another function was to direct an individual's thoughts and actions by its (moral) authority. Therefore, for some individuals who have a particular religious belief, personal choice may not enter into the framework for the generation of options. The religious framework is a mechanism for decision-making. Decision-making out of, or in conflict with, the religious framework may introduce deep personal conflict and evoke guilt due to 'unacceptable' options being acted upon or pursued.

Pederson believes that spiritual and religious factors are important for the counsellor in providing a foundation of cultural and value differences between them and their clients. As with other areas of counsellor–client difference, religious differences may be dismissed, ignored or minimized by counsellors. To avoid these pitfalls, Worthington (1989) has identified 4 factors to bring to counsellors' attention regarding religion and the counsellor's direct work with a client.

1. A high proportion of the population identifies themselves as having some form of religious belief.
2. It appears that many people who are undergoing emotional crises spontaneously consider religion in their considerations of their difficulty.
3. Some clients are reluctant to bring up religious issues because of perceptions that therapy is a secular experience.
4. Counsellors tend not to be as religiously oriented as clients (Pate and Bondi, 1992).

Counsellors who are less religiously oriented than their clients may tend not to be as well informed, about religious belief and its influence on an individual's life and the counselling process, as may be necessary when considering the needs of religious clients.

In considering the impact of religion in the counselling process, it is useful to ask 'What is the incidence of religious belief in Britain?' In Britain the available cross-cultural survey evidence (Modood et al., 1998) suggests that religion is central in the identity and self-definition of most South Asian people. For most South Asian groups, only 2 per cent claimed to have no religion although with people of Indian, as opposed to Pakistani and Bangladeshi background, the proportion rose to 5 per cent who claimed to have no religion. More than half of the Chinese people sampled claimed not to have a religion. Also, half of the sample of white people in Britain aged 16 to 34 claimed to have no religion. In this research, gender was also seen to be a factor, with women more likely to have a religion, particularly amongst African-Caribbean women where 75 per cent of African-Caribbean women claimed to have a religious belief and less than two-thirds of African-Caribbean men claimed that they had no religious beliefs. Among the total (all ages) white respondents in the survey, 31 per cent claimed to have no religious connection, although this figure reduced to less than half with the white Irish sample. This research reveals that the chance of encountering an individual in counselling who has religious beliefs is high.

Boyd-Franklyn (1989) has suggested that when working with black people, difficulties will sometimes be framed in religious terms as a metaphor. This may be a way of testing to see if the counsellor is in tune and understands and respects their beliefs. Religion affects the options and behaviour people see themselves as having, much in the same way that culture has an influence. For example, a Roman Catholic may not see abortion as an option when discovering they have an unwanted pregnancy. A Muslim woman or man may experience personal conflict or guilt with a group of non-Muslim friends who wish to go to a pub for entertainment and fear loss of friendship networks unless they review their beliefs.

Religion and culture – related, but not synonymous

In considering religion and its significance in the counselling process, it is important that the counsellor realizes that religion and culture, although related, are not synonymous. Culture affects religion but religion also influences culture. For example, the religious practices of African-Caribbean Christians may be very different to that of white British Christians both in terms of religious belief and in terms of culture. Likewise, whereas it may be inappropriate to shake the hand of a Muslim Pakistani woman if the counsellor is of the opposite gender, it would be seen as bad manners if a counsellor did not shake the hand of a Sudanese Muslim woman irrespective of the counsellor's gender. It is not enough to know the religion of the person and believe that one understands an individual's cultural beliefs and behaviour. Religions may be shared by people from many different cultural and ethnic groups who have different cultural behaviours. However, it may also be argued that religion influences and affects culture to such a degree that it can change belief and practice both over time and from one culture to another.

In the same way that the counsellor should not attempt to 'separate' an individual from their culture during counselling, neither should a counsellor attempt to 'separate' a client from their religious beliefs. For some individuals religious belief is of fundamental importance in self-definition. Rosenblat argues that one should not fall into the trap of viewing what is termed in the west as religion as an easily mapped construct into the beliefs of other cultures. In holding this faulty view there may arise a set of ethnocentric beliefs about the nature of the world and the relationship of the living with the dead. In the context of counselling Rosenblat argues that

> the grief of someone from a culture where the emotions of bereavement are quite different from those in one's own culture may seem insincere or artificial, or may even seem to result from a failure to understand what death really is. A westerner may have trouble understanding and accepting a grief heavily laden with joking and laughter, murderous rage, wailing and lamentation that go on for months or mute unresponsiveness. However, for the bereaved, the expression of emotions may be totally sincere and heartfelt, may fit what that person understands about death and grief, and it is likely to be, for that person, the most desirable way to act. (1997: 36)

Thus, just in the way that culture can shape behaviour, so too can religious belief, as it affects social ritual and understanding of death and bereavement, and the display of grief that an individual presents in the counselling scenario. The counsellor will therefore need to be in tune with their own cultural and (non-)religious preoccupations and assumptions surrounding religion and its expression.

How religion might affect the counselling process

First, just as culture is of key significance in coming to an understanding about an individual's perception of their experience and the events that bring them into counselling, religion too can have this affect. For example, in the video series 'Counselling Black Clients in Britain' (Banks, 1992) there is a scene used for counselling training, which considers the position of an adolescent Sikh male who believes that to become attractive to girls and get a girlfriend, he must cut his hair and dispense with the wearing of his turban. The counsellor explores the meaning of this religious/cultural symbolism in the young man's understanding and also in his family's understanding. This is done in the context of not only what the removal of the turban and cutting of the man's hair will mean to himself, but also what it will mean to his family and his relationship with his family and community. Consider what your response would be to a young Sikh who comes to you for counselling with this issue. How capable would you see yourself of dealing with this young man's dilemma without a knowledge and understanding of the cultural, religious and spiritual significance of the man's turban? Would it be adequate, given the cultural and religious significance to only explore and pursue the young man's view and wishes outside of the influence of religion and culture? If so, one may be working with guilt-invoking temptations, rather than deeply held convictions about the need for a girlfriend. In this context, restricting the counselling focus to matters of individualized needs and wants is unlikely to help the young man achieve a satisfactory outcome. This would be much too narrow and blinkered a process.

Raising issues of religion and culture with clients

Many counsellors may argue that it is for the client to raise the significance of external factors in the counselling process. However, as Worthington (1989) has argued, this rarely happens when influences in the client's life are religious, as clients tend to believe that the counselling arena is secular. This behaviour may arise in some cases from a desire of the client's to protect the counsellor from discovery of his or her own ignorance. The counselling may proceed in a less than informed way in its lack of account of what may be a major influence on a client's way of understanding and construing the world. Given the likelihood that most of Worthington's focus was work with Christians, the counsellor must ask him/herself how much this assertion by Worthington is likely to be true when working with non-Christian groups. It may well be that the client enters the counselling arena, particularly where the counsellor is white, with a belief that the counsellor knows nothing about the client's religion (even considering that it may not be recognized at all). For some clients, this may be a wish to consider their position out of a religious context and they may seek out counsellors who are not of the same religious orientation as them. What the counsellor must consider is whether this is an acceptable means by which to achieve a satisfactory outcome for the client. It is the counsellor's professional duty to enable the client to consider all angles of their situation in order for them to achieve a satisfactory outcome. A counselling encounter which does not seek to acknowledge all aspects of an individual's being can be considered as mono-dimensional and not representative of the sum of parts that constitute that individual and their options for response to their difficulties. In the video training trigger scene of the young Sikh man, the counsellor reaches an awareness that in order to progress the central question of the client's, it is important for them both to work within a religious influence context. This awareness is facilitated in the client and achieved by the counsellor with the result that the counsellor makes the suggestion that he try to find, within the counselling service, an individual who is knowledgeable about Sikhism and that the young Sikh man has further sessions with this individual. The counsellor, having acknowledged his/her ignorance of a key factor necessary to help the client explore their options, suggests referral to another counsellor, which the client accepted. There may be times when referral to an individual of the same religion is appropriate just as there may be times when this is not appropriate. The client best judges the measure of appropriateness. For example, consider the situation where a young woman presents as being pregnant, unmarried, part way through a university course and highly stressed as to what to do. She sees herself as having no choices, as her religious belief is one that does not allow children outside of marriage and neither does it allow her the option of having an abortion. The woman also brings into the conversation the shame and pressure that will result from her pregnancy in the perception of her community and her family. At this point it is not necessary to be specific about the exact religion of the female client. She could be a Muslim or a Catholic. The counsellor should also be aware that sometimes it is difficult to 'disentangle' religious belief from personal belief. The personal belief of an individual that all life is sacred, and the view that religion views all life as sacred may mean that the lack of abortion option is seen as having a religious foundation. In these circumstances it may be that the female client believes her only option is to consider her position outside of a religious context, to remove what she may perceive as pressure to conform to a set of expectations that do not allow her the degree of open-endedness that she wishes. It should be questioned whether religion allows a client options or whether religion only offers a set of prescribed, narrowly defined 'options' heavily influenced by dogma which increases a client's anxiety when the beliefs do not fit with emotional need or cognitive appraisal of necessary action. It may be that the influence of dogma is a false belief of the individual or the religious leaders of the client who interpret religious practice in too narrow a way. However, one should be aware that the 'virginity principle' may apply here. For example, one transgression of religious belief may permanently remove the individual from attachment to their religious identity and the one transgression (pregnancy out of marriage) may be the first in a number of steps down the path of distance from group membership. This may, for some individuals who are dependant on this for their core identity, have very serious consequences at both a psychological and practical social survival level.

After counselling, it may be that the female client reaches the same decision that she would have reached with a counsellor of the same religious orientation, but the degree of satisfaction of her chosen direction may be greater as she has achieved her decision and direction through reflection on her own individualized needs and beliefs rather than feeling that she was unduly influenced by a counsellor or a process that can only take religious doctrine into account. However, behaviour determined by religion may require continuity to support self-definition and individual belongingness. In this counselling dilemma, where a counsellor takes the view that abortion is a wholly acceptable option that should be considered without guilt, it would be necessary to consider how this value is conveyed to the client and the effect that this has on the counselling process. The counsellor too may have religious values. The counsellor should ask him/herself whether, in effect, the counselling becomes so value-laden that it becomes a proselytising activity where an attempt is made to convert the client to a belief and value system that does not easily fit that which the client entered the counselling arena with. There are many subjects such as contraception and sexuality for example, that are likely to raise differences in opinion and basic values in the counselling scenario between client and counsellor. It may be that until some of these topics are encountered from a differing perspective than their own, counsellors do not recognize how strongly held their values are. Meeting an individual whose values are different may raise issues of personal belief challenge for the counsellor.

Reflexive practice

Just as a counsellor who has religious values is likely to need to self-assess how these impact in the counselling scenario, the counsellor who professes to have no religious values is also likely to need to consider how their past learnings affect their work with clients whose religious values and dilemmas are made explicit. For example, in a recent counsellor training course, the case study of a woman described as having 'strong religious beliefs' was presented. This case study involved a woman with two children who came to counselling with feelings of isolation and estrangement. In counselling, the woman's religious beliefs arose and the counsellor found that the woman believed that she must put up with the neglect of her emotional needs from her husband and her young teenage children, as 'one is put on this earth to suffer and through suffering one will find the true meaning of God.' This case study triggered many angry feelings in the counselling training participants, particularly those with feminist principles. For other trainees, there arose during discussion, personal difficulties around religious beliefs as they themselves were raised in what they described as 'religious families'. These trainees had believed that their environment had been repressive and had stunted their emotional development. They openly stated that they had 'no time for religious nutters'. This hostile and dismissive attitude is likely to show itself in the counselling environment and negatively affect the relationship with the client, the process and outcome of counselling. The identified intolerance that the trainees displayed enabled them, in the training scenario, to be placed in a position to consider and reflect on how their views would impact on their work with the client. However, for a few, the impact of this work was such that they openly admitted being unable to pursue work with this client due to their own experiences of religion and religious teaching in their early and late childhood. This had left them with bitter resentment towards those who clung to religion and its practices. A heated debate arose in which others attempted to get the dismissive individuals to reflect on whether their experience was unfortunate and distorted and whether this could be generalized to the experience of all. However, such was the strength of feeling that in some cases this self-reflection was not possible. For counsellors who are unable to accept the importance of religion in a client's day-to-day life, it may be that they need to review this resistance to achieve a cognitive shift to consider the influence of this perspective on an individual's 'world view'. Sue & Sue (1990) see a world view as a holistic construct that integrates the belief systems, values, lifestyles and modes of problem solving that are specific to a particular group. For some groups there will be what is called an internal locus of control in which outcomes are based on a person's own actions and, for others, an external locus of control in which outcomes are believed to result from luck, chance or fate (Rotter, 1975). Sue & Sue have further developed these notions and added an internal locus of responsibility where success or lack of success in a desired goal is attributed to a person's skills resulting in either self blame or blame of another. With an external locus of responsibility, the environmental factors are seen as more potent than individual factors and result in system blame. It is possible that those clients who have strong religious beliefs are likely to be high on the external locus of control variable, and this will influence the options people see themselves as having in counselling and how the counselling process should proceed.

As has been said, some individuals' moral code, options of choice and resultant behaviour are determined by religious belief. It is not for the counsellor to dismiss or minimize the importance of this way of construing the world. Religion is but one aspect of difference that needs to be shown respect and tolerance. The counsellor working within an anti-oppressive practice framework will have respect and due consideration for difference at every level. Counsellors who claim to have no religious belief may need to reflect whether their own counselling orientation and its influence on their world view and values is, in effect, a form of religious belief. Certainly this has been questioned by me as I hear individuals compare the 'value' of their counselling orientation to that of others. Perhaps counselling, for some, fulfils the place of religion?

Some ideas for good practice:

- Explore, through self-reflection and good supervision, your attitudes towards religious and cultural practices which do not 'fit' with your own values.
- Be mindful and respectful of the fundamental part religion and culture might play in a client's identity.
- Question your own resistance to accepting others' cultural and religious beliefs.
- Consider referral to another counsellor should you and your client be unable to 'meet' in relation to issues of religion or culture, so that the client may receive an optimum opportunity for empathy.
- Consider the use of consultation or undertake some research to gain some knowledge of the difficulties clients might be working on.

References

Banks, N.J. (1992) *Counselling Black Clients in Britain*. The University of Birmingham, UK: Television and Media Department.

Boyd-Franklyn, N. (1989) *Black Families in Therapy: A Multi-Systems Approach*. New York: Guilford.

Freud, S. (1921) *Group Psychology and the Analysis of the Ego*. Penguin Freud Library, Vol. 12.

Jacobs, M. (1992) *Sigmund Freud*. London: Sage.

Modood, T., Berthoud, R., Lakey, J., Nazroo, J., Smith, P., Virdee, S., & Beishon, S. (1998) *Ethnic Minorities in Britain, Diversity and Disadvantage*. Policy Studies Institute.

Pate, R.H. & Bondi, A.M. (1992) 'Religious Beliefs and Practice: An Integral Aspect of Modern Cultural Awareness,' *Counselor Education and Supervision*, 32, pp. 108–115.

Pedersen, P.B. (1997) *Culture Centered Counselling Interventions – Striving for Accuracy*. Thousand Oaks, CA: Sage.

Rotter, J. (1975) 'Some Problems and Misconceptions Related to the Construct of Internal versus External Control of Reinforcement', *Journal of Consulting and Clinical Psychology*, 43, pp. 56–67.

Sue, D.W. & Sue, D. (1990) *Counseling the Culturally Different* (second edition). New York: Wiley.

Worthington, E.L. (1989) 'Religious Faith across the Lifespan,' *The Counselling Psychologist*, 17(4), pp. 555–612.

9   *Class and Counselling*

Anne Kearney

Recent writing for counselling/therapy has addressed itself to developing a greater understanding of different types of oppression, which are part of our social world. This chapter looks at an aspect of potential oppression which is largely ignored in such discussions – that of social class. Giddens invites us to consider 'two phenomena, which should be conceptually separate – *class and class consciousness*. Class differences exist regardless of whether people are conscious of them' (1993: 227). Dominelli, writing about racism in social work describes a 'colour-blind approach' where white workers ignore the colour of black people's skin. 'It is not that they are unaware of the colour of a person's skin, but that they discount its significance' (1988: 36). I am suggesting here that this equally applies to class, and that the counselling profession and its members are largely 'class-blind'. This chapter is an invitation to confront our class-blindness and consider the implications of class difference in our counselling, supervision and training activities.

Class differences

Controversy surrounds most discussions of class within the social sciences where there is frequent disagreement between protagonists as to what social class actually is. The theoretical disagreements between researchers, whilst relevant, are not the focus of this chapter, though I have discussed them in greater detail elsewhere (Kearney, 1996).

There are three main approaches to discussions about social class. The first, that of Karl Marx, is based on the ownership of wealth (capital, as he calls it). There are two major groupings of people in society, he argues;

those who own capital and those who do not – the bourgeoisie and the proletariat. Those who own capital in the form of land, plant and equipment employ those who do not. They exploit workers through making profit from their labour and pay them as little as they can get away with. Apart from the two major groupings, Marx identified two other groupings, much smaller in number than the bourgeoisie or the proletariat. These are what he called the 'intermediate classes' and the 'lumpen proletariat', what present day writers sometimes refer to as the 'underclass' who are neither owners of capital, nor are they employed by owners.

The second major description of social class is given by Max Weber who, though he did not disagree with Marx, did feel that Marx's description 'missed out' some important features of class – such as status and power. Weber saw the class system as being similar to a ladder, with a different group on each step. The steps differ from each other not only in terms of wealth, but in terms of lifestyle, status and the amount of power they have. This seems superficially to be very different from Marx's view, but like Marx, Weber claimed that it is wealth and our position on the ladder that determines our 'life chances' (our experiences, opportunities) and general 'way of being'.

The third approach to describing the class system is not a historical one, it is rather a 'snapshot' description of what the class system looks like in terms of the ladder or hierarchy as described by Weber. This view – the Registrar General's classification of social class – looks at the occupational system and categorizes people on the basis of the job they do. It consists of 5 main groupings of jobs arranged on a hierarchy from the 'top' jobs, such as lawyers and doctors, to the 'bottom' jobs such as unskilled labourers. It is basically a bureaucratic view of social class, designed to provide administrative and policy guidelines (such as the number of council houses we may need to build), rather than an attempt to understand the class system, as Marx and Weber were trying to do.

As such, the Registrar General's categorization of jobs has limited use as an aid to understanding; it is based on the Head of Household for instance, and makes no reference to people who are not in the occupational system, such as unemployed people or those with full-time care obligations.

For the purpose of this discussion I am using a very broad definition of class which is fairly arbitrary. I am using the concepts of 'middle class' and 'working class' to describe the differences between those people who, while they are not owners of wealth, in Marx's terms, do occupy different positions in the class structure. By 'middle class' I mean those people who do 'white collar' jobs as distinct from those who do 'blue-collar' (or manual jobs). I am aware of the crudeness of this distinction, in that there are many variations of income, status and power *within* each of these groups. Nevertheless, research suggests that the great divide is between those who do non-manual and those who do manual work. I am also aware that the most deprived and disadvantaged people are those who, for whatever reason, have no job and that in recent years this group has massively grown. That unemployment itself creates deprivation and consequently psychological problems for people is not in question. There is no doubt whatever in my mind that the constraints imposed by unemployment and poverty directly and indirectly create and sustain emotional difficulties for people. I suggest that they are difficulties which are different in degree rather than in kind from those of employed people who are exploited and impoverished – and often disenfranchised, too. These difficulties include problems of ego development, poor self-esteem, feelings of unworthiness, self-loathing and shame.

Social class is a major determinant of our life experiences. Our socioeconomic position, and consequent life-style, our values, attitudes and traditions, and our life chances all impact on who we become and what we might bring to therapy. It is well documented that income, standard of education, language use, health and leisure opportunities are all influenced by the class position that we occupy. There is general agreement that there are huge disparities of power, status and money between the two major classes and that each of us is positioned in either one or the other grouping (Hutton, 1995). I am suggesting here that it is these very things that often *create* the conditions that bring clients to counselling.

The impact of class difference on the counselling profession and on clients

Class and counsellor training

On beginning counsellor training we are embarking on a process of acquiring skills, knowledge and values, which form the basis of our 'expertise'. Training has already been contaminated, however, by class issues in a number of ways:

- Most trainers occupy middle class positions which give them social power by virtue of their role.
- Trainees are disproportionately middle class, since training is expensive and many cannot access it.
- The training itself is influenced by predominantly middle class assumptions and values which are rarely explored during the course.

- The emphasis on individualism, personal choice and personal responsibility are informed by (and in their turn form) an ethos of training which is class-based.

These factors have very direct consequences for *all* trainees whether middle class or working class. For middle class trainees it may result in their not being challenged and invited to explore the class based assumptions they may (unwittingly) hold about people and which may impact on their future work with clients. The impact on working class trainees is different but equally important. I offer an example from my own practice when a trainee in supervision said 'I feel I don't know anything about people any more, and I always thought I was perceptive'. What emerged on further exploration was her sense that her 'knowledge' of people was valued less highly than 'knowledge' being exhibited by other trainees from more prestigious social class backgrounds.

We can gain 'knowledge' in a number of ways; by experience, by observation, by intuition, by being 'given' it, or by reading. We tend to assume that there is an absolute difference between what is 'known' publicly (in other words, what people generally agree is the case) and what we know privately, from 'gut feeling', personal experience or personal observation. It is very likely that those people who share a similar class position will observe and experience in broadly similar ways and this becomes the 'knowledge' that this group share in a taken-for-granted way. It is at this point that social power differences become very important because the shared 'knowledge' of middle class people is imbued with the greater authority allocated to them in class terms. It is middle class perceptions, middle class experiences and middle class interpretations which are seen to *be* knowledge and working class knowledge is thereby demoted to 'folklore' or 'being canny'. A similar process takes place between women and men, where 'men's knowledge' is seen as superior to 'women's knowledge' which is demoted and devalued as inferior.

I suggest that what passes for 'knowledge' is socially constructed and is widely influenced by social class considerations. I prefer to think that there are 'knowledges', rather than only one legitimate 'knowledge'. In the process of knowledge construction the greater power and status attributed to being middle class promotes certain kinds of knowledge and legitimizes it over others. What this trainee was expressing was her internalized devaluing of her own knowledge – her perception and intuition – ironically a fundamental quality for counsellors.

Ideally, there should be no need on any training course to address issues of oppression on the basis of gender, class and race, etc., as 'add on' modules. These would all be dealt with in the main body of the training and would be central to it. While there is now a growing volume of work and literature on, for example, transcultural counselling (Pedersen and Ivey, 1994; Lago & Thompson, 1996) there is no specific attention paid to class as an external form of oppression. Our awareness of class as a major source of oppression in therapeutic work seems less advanced than our awareness of other types of oppression and seems to be less well understood in its detail than other forms.

What I am claiming here is that the training world of counselling/ psychotherapy operates from essentially middle class assumptions and values, assumptions that are rarely (if ever) challenged, and perceived to be apolitical and universal. It may be difficult for individual trainees to challenge the ideological basis of their training where the very people doing the training are those who will assess and judge their work and who probably belong to professional organizations which fail to challenge the underlying premises of the work they legitimize. In other words the counselling community, as trainers, counsellors and supervisors, seems reluctant to recognize that we as a profession are positioned in a wider world where inequalities are normalized and taken for granted. We take a stance (by default, if not actively) in relation to these inequalities – a stance that either challenges them (both as professionals and as citizens) or endorses them by our *failure* to challenge them.

One of the outcomes of this for working class counsellors is a feeling expressed by one training supervisee that he felt 'silenced' by a sense of alienation from the very 'middle class niceness' that he experienced in his training. His concerns were as much with what was missing from his training – its absences – as with what was present. He had come from a world where poverty was a daily struggle for most people he knew, to one where poverty was rarely, if ever, mentioned. His community of origin was one in which poor housing and irresponsible landlords were part of the everyday experiences of people, yet awareness of these experiences was 'absent from his training'. He withdrew from his training on the grounds that 'counselling is not about people like me, we don't figure'.

Clients, shame and class

The counselling community's failure to confront class inequalities and the different experiences of class disadvantaged people (trainees as well as clients) results in counselling becoming an elite activity, aimed at other privileged people whilst paying lip service to the equal value of every unique individual, at odds with the actual day-to-day practice of counselling/psychotherapy. This is not to doubt the integrity of individual trainers and therapists, but to argue that our reluctance as a professional group to take on the difficulties and challenges of these aspects of our work and to see them as having relevance to oppressed people may well result in our being part of the process of oppression (Hutton, 1995).

In the remainder of this chapter I want to explore the actual ways in which the 'class-blind' approach to our work may impact on clients, in particular where the client is working class and the counsellor/psychotherapist is middle class. I will examine some of the areas where I believe the impact may be greatest, though the areas I have selected are illustrative and not exhaustive.

From the moment the client makes contact with us, our class differences or similarities are apparent – and significant. Our initial contact may be either by telephone or (in the case of GP or other organizational settings) they may involve face-to-face contact which gives more visual 'clues'. Telephone contact draws attention to accent, language use, the degree of warmth and/or formality and will mobilize a whole set of stereotypic assumptions on both sides which may facilitate or hinder further contact. A middle class accent and use of language may reinforce a working class client's internalized classism and the same process may be activated for the counsellor. Middle class accents and language use are differently powered; they are perceived as 'superior', as having status and as conveying 'expertness' which in turn may add to the power imbalances between the counsellor (who is likely to be skilled and experienced at making verbal contact with clients) and a client who may be feeling anxious and vulnerable anyway. A very perceptive and able working class client recently said to me 'as soon as I heard you, I knew you'd know how to help me, I knew you'd know what to do'. Processing this when the client came for her session enabled us both to separate out the impact of my middle class accent and her class-based assumption that middle class people automatically 'know best' and in so doing, we could talk very early on about the power issues which were an important theme in her therapeutic work. It can operate in the other direction too. As a client said in her first review 'I wasn't sure I'd be able to tell you the things I needed to, you might be shocked, you might think I was awful'. Again, processing this enabled both of us to be aware of the class differences between us and how they might impede (or enhance) our work together.

The settings in which we work also make statements about class differences. I am aware for instance, in my GP based work, that the medical setting contributes to a sense of class difference, particularly for working class clients. There seems to be a 'spin-off effect' of status from the doctors in the surgery to me, so clients have a tendency at first to be more distant and formal when saying why they have come. The medical setting seems to have the effect of clients describing their lives in terms of 'symptoms' and to feel, at least initially, that they cannot be 'real' with me.

When I work from home the setting is still not free from class clues and clients will often make comments which outline this; 'have you read all those books?' These observations present us with ideal opportunities to explore the client's underlying assumptions and their own and my own class positions, which I believe have a definite impact on the therapeutic work.

I have become convinced that these differences have an impact on how we, as counsellors, actually hear clients and how they hear us. Given that middle class language (i.e. Bernstien's 'elaborated code', 1971) is more highly valued generally, the client may feel doubly disempowered by the differences between us. In the first place I, as a middle class woman, will selectively choose what parts of the client's content to reflect back. In doing that I may unwittingly be attributing a middle class meaning structure to what has been said and, when that is combined with the already existing power differences between the client and myself, the chances that the client will feel empowered enough to challenge my understanding are greatly diminished.

When we fail to take into account that this might happen, we take the risk of 'missing' the client (Hargaden & Summers, 2000). These authors cite the work of Sterne who gives the example of client X who was brought up in a working class family. X tells the therapist of an incident that she knows happened when she was an infant but does not have a memory of.

'X: 'My parents came to collect me from the hospital but I did not recognize them. I just sat between them sighing (sounds sad and a little lost) … I had lost them forever…'

Therapist: 'That little baby, sitting there, feeling lost and hurt, sitting in the car between her mummy and daddy but not knowing that they were her mummy and daddy.' Upon hearing the word 'car', X froze and felt embarrassed. Her family had never owned a car and her parents could not drive. She felt paralyzed by a sense of shame and confusion. (1985: 153).

The client's story and its attendant feelings are at risk, then, of becoming a multi-layered process of self-rebuke by the climate in which s/he sees him/herself as somehow 'lacking' something. Of course, the 'lack' in the case of working class clients is that of a middle class framework within which to interpret experiences. For the counsellor, too, there is a lack – of a working-class framework. But the therapeutic setting is not an objective area where different frameworks compete on equal terms when class differences exist between therapist/client. It is an area in which the therapist's framework is given much greater legitimacy by virtue of his/her 'expertise' and, just as importantly (and maybe even more so) by virtue of his/her 'middle-classness'. In other words what happens in the therapy room parallels what happens in the outside world – middle class people are given (and internalize) greater status, power and authority than working class people.

One consequence of this is that it can (and I suspect, often does) result in the counsellor/therapist holding (probably unconsciously) a 'deficit model' of the client. The client may be seen as being deficient in experiences or deficient in insight or even deficient in feeling when compared with the therapist's own measures. Of course, from the perspective of the client, the same would be the case from his/her perspective, the counsellor/therapist could be seen as deficient in the area of experience, knowledge and even feelings that the client has. Again, this might not seem to matter too much; after all, this happens very commonly when people from different backgrounds interact socially. But it does matter – greatly – in the therapeutic context where the therapist/counsellor is already more powerful than the client and where it is the job of the therapist to enter into the meaning structure of the client – on the client's terms. It is almost impossible for this to be achieved if the therapist fails to take account of and raise awareness of the class differences between them. The failure to do that creates the risk that the client believes him/herself to be 'wrong' in some way; to somehow not be feeling what s/he 'should' be feeling. It is too big a responsibility to impose on the client the expectation that s/he will 'hold on to' his/her sense of self, experiences and interpretations when they are not being validated by the therapist. This is the therapist's responsibility and it is one that most of our training and our professional organization fails to prepare us for. Unless we become and remain aware that social class structures our experience and expectation and greatly informs our learning framework we run the risk of inaccurately imputing meaning to the client's story. If we are unaware of the impact of social class we may not be alert to the potential 'mis-hearing' and/or misunderstanding, and the distance between us and the client becomes greater.

This could be avoided if training involved a component which required trainees to become familiar with the relevant information about how society is organized, how social class operates and how power inequalities are created and sustained by such divisions. Let us take, for example, the experience of counsellors in prisons or in drug counselling agencies, which are largely populated by working class clients. It is important to question what part social class played in each of the lives of these clients. What cultural and socio-economic influences, for example locality, poor housing, peer group, poor education, unemployment and poverty were the backdrop to *this* client's story and their current situation?

Summary

The different class contexts of people's lives have a direct effect on client/counsellor interactions in a number of ways. Financial status is one of these. In terms of income, many of the class differences have been eroded since the post-war years. The *average* gap in income between the two main classes has *on average* reduced when we measure those in full employment. This is not so for individual working class or middle class people; poverty is a major problem for very many families and individuals. While it is not the case that all working class people are poor, the majority of those people who are poor are working class. This directly affects the availability of counselling – the general rule is that the poorer you are, the less chance there is that you will have access to counselling, and that when you do, usually through the NHS or a charitable organization, the choices you have are very limited. A poor working class client 'gets who they get' – s/he cannot choose the type of therapy/counselling, the setting, the duration or the actual person involved. A fee-paying client can choose each one of these.

I have chosen to examine just a few of the ways in which social class impacts on our training and counselling. I would like to consider here why this should happen and what it is that prevents the counselling profession from recognizing the situation and taking some action.

Counselling/therapy draws on and recruits people who are very disparate in a number of ways. On any counselling training course the age range is quite wide and the occupational background of trainees is varied. What they all share in common, though, is a commitment to developing 'helping relationships' with people and groups. One of the ways in which the disparate elements of a training group develops cohesion is by emphasizing the shared aspects of the group and thereby enhancing just that. The negative aspect of this is that differences between group members tend to be 'down-played' and the external world (in which these differences are important) is relatively ignored, emphasizing the individual, not the social. The attention to the 'purely' individual aspects of people seem to preclude attention to the social contexts of those individuals' lives and (though this may not be at all the trainer's intention) what trainees learn is that we can safely ignore those contexts since they are not directly relevant to counselling/therapy. In other words, part of what we are being 'trained into' is an ideology which suggests that counsellors/therapists can pursue their work without needing to know or understand much about clients' lives outside the counselling relationship, except what the client tells them. Much of what influences us is so taken for granted by us that it seems like a 'given' and so self-evident that it does not need to even be mentioned. In terms of the establishment, counselling/therapy are much more likely to become more securely part of the mainstream if we do not rock the boat politically; if we remain 'above' disagreements about politics and if we do not encourage our clients to question the power inequalities that limit their lives. Unless we have addressed these issues within our profession and in ourselves, – questioned our own position by way of privilege or disadvantage – we cannot assume a readiness to support our clients in their own journey to awareness and healing.

Some key issues

- Familiarize ourselves with the social and political influences which bring clients to counselling.
- Be aware of our own class background and the privileges or disadvantages which came with that.
- Recognize that knowledge is power and that working class clients may not know that their experiences and opportunities have been influenced by class position.
- Be aware that the historical development and current ethos of counselling is one which elevates middle class knowledge and experience to the status of universal truths.
- Recognize, acknowledge and process with clients the fact that our class position has psychological as well as social consequences. We may feel shame, embarrassment, inferiority and self consciousness.
- Consider a sliding scale for fees if working privately.
- Raise awareness of class issues with colleagues if working for an agency.

References

Bernstein, B. (1971) *Class, Codes and Control*. Vol. 1. London: Routledge and Kegan Paul.
Dominelli, L. (1988) *Anti-Racist Social Work*. London: Macmillan.

Giddens, A. (1993) *Sociology* (second edition). Cambridge: Polity Press.

Hargaden, H. & Summers, G. (2000) 'Class, Shame and Self-righteousness', in Conference Papers *Embracing Life's Differences*. ITA Conference, 2000.

Hutton, W. (1995) *The State We're In*. London: Johnathan Cape.

Kearney, A. (1996) *Counselling, Class and Politics – Undeclared Influences in Therapy*. Manchester: PCCS Books.

Lago, C. & Thompson, J. (1996) *Race, Culture and Counselling*. Buckingham: Open University.

Pedersen, P. & Ivey, A.E. (1994) *Culture-Centered Counseling and Interviewing Skills*. Westpoint, CT: Greenwood/Preager.

Sterne, D.N. (1985) *The Interpersonal World of the Infant*. New York: Basic Books.

10   *Double, Triple, Multiple Jeopardy*

Roy Moodley

The post-structuralist and modernist view seems to suggest that an individual's subjectivity is a construction of his or her socio-cultural and psychosocial environments within which issues of gender, race[1], ethnicity, class, disability and sexual orientation[2] tend to play a critical role. The notion of plural or multiple identities is now more acceptable and takes precedence over the conventional idea that a person's identity is singular, fixed or static. In this chapter I want to consider how these multiple social and cultural identities are understood, experienced and 'worked with' in counselling. For example, what happens in the therapeutic relationship with a client who may be black and disabled? Would issues of race take precedence over being deaf? Or if a client were gay would this be privileged over issues of race or class? In other words, what happens to clients who disclose one of the multi(ple) cultural identities (class, gender, race, sexual orientation) but not the other/s? Can an authentic therapeutic relationship be experienced with one or the other of their identities being marginalized and rendered invisible, and with the client feeling oppressed through this experience? Can the present practice of counselling cope with the multiple cultural identities that may be disclosed and shared in therapy? Or are these clients in double, triple or multiple jeopardy?

This chapter sets out to explore these questions in the following ways: First, by considering the constructions of double, triple and multiple jeopardy in relation to the social categories of race, gender, class, disability and sexual orientation. Second, it examines the problematic of the 'other'[3] to suggest that there is no hierarchy in terms of race, gender, class, disability and sexual orientation. Through a brief examination of the current practice of counselling the chapter considers therapists' attitude towards the 'other', and asks whether the present multi(ple) cultural therapies can comprehend the complexity of experiencing that goes on in clients who feel multiple oppression. The chapter concludes with a look at the strategies clients adopt in therapy to understand their multiple oppressions.

Constructions of double, triple, multi(ple)cultural jeopardy

The term 'double jeopardy' was initially put forward by the National Urban League (1964) in the USA, to express the two-fold discrimination of *age* and *race* and focused on the disadvantages of income and ill health experienced by older black people (Blakemore and Boneham, 1994). Since then a number of researchers have attempted to define the term in different ways. For example, Jenness sees 'double jeopardy' as oppression of black women in terms of 'anti-women criminal code abortion laws; unequal pay; jobs; and educational opportunities; denial of adequate community controlled child care; and so on' (1972: 40). In Britain, the term is used rather loosely to refer to race, class, gender discrimination and more. For example, Alison Norman says,

> The acuteness of the isolation of those who by reason of language, culture, skin colour or religious belief find themselves unable to gain access to treatment, support and care … They are not merely in double jeopardy by reason of age and discrimination … but in triple jeopardy, at risk because they are old, because of the physical conditions and hostility under which they live, *and* because services are not accessible to them. (1985: 1). [Italics in original]

Thus we see that 'triple jeopardy' evolved to refer to the combined impact of race, age and *social class* – or as Paz and Aleman (1998) put it: being old, poor and a member of a minority group. According to Blakemore and Boneham (1994), multiple hazards indicate an even more disadvantaged position resulting from other factors such as sex discrimination. In a recent paper, 'Multiple Jeopardy: Risk and protective factors amongst addicted mothers' offsprings' Luthar et al. (1998) attempted to consider age, ethnicity, race, severity of maternal psychiatric disturbance and higher and lower child mental cognitive abilities. It seems then, that the definition of the numerically accumulating jeopardy is able to accommodate the newer forms and formulation of discrimination that arise in society. In keeping with this tradition of the changing nature of the concept, I have included disability and sexual orientations as part of the debate on multiple discriminations in counselling.

Therefore, in this chapter, double, triple or multiple jeopardy refers to race, gender, class, sexual orientation and disability discrimination which the multi(ple) cultural 'other' – the disabled, the gay, the lesbian, hetero-sexual women, working-class clients – experience as 'otherness'[4] in their day-to-day living. A lack of knowing/knowledge can easily lead a thera-pist to assume that the effects of individual oppressions may be cumula-tive rather than complex and confounding. Examining these issues is more than looking at the facts of discrimination. It may be, as Blakemore and Boneham (1994) suggest, about establishing theory, building hypo-thesis and developing a more sensitive recognition of people who experi-ence these discriminations. Most research and theorization of these issues in counselling has examined the individual effects of racism, anti-Semitism, sexism, disabilism, homophobia and ageism on the physical and mental (ill) health of the individual. The effects of a combination of these experiences have not been researched adequately nor given much attention in the counselling literature. We still know very little about the complexity of affective experiencing that takes place when these oppres-sions act together. In social science, however, where these issues are beginning to be interrogated, black feminists such as Lorde (1984), have emphasized the various ways in which racism, anti-Semitism, sexism, dis-abilism, homophobia and ageism interconnect and overlap as agents of oppression.

No hierarchy in the 'other' category: race, gender, class, disability, sexual orientations

Postmoderism appears to indicate that notions such as race, gender, class, disability and sexual orientation are not fixed, transhistorical or essential-ist, but are flexible, dynamic and multiple. An individual's identity is a mixture of his or her gender, race, ethnic, class and sexual orientation identity, and no one identity takes precedence over the other in an individual's inner world. If all these discursive practices are influential in the personality make-up of the individual, then it seems reasonable to assume that in counselling a client who chooses to disclose one or more of their multi(ple) cultural identities, in different moments and move-ments in therapy, is undertaking this process to answer ontological and existential questions.

The representation, presentation and interpretation of one's identity in therapy is always a complex issue and a number of variables may act and interact together to produce a particular transference relationship. Being black, or deaf, or gay, or lesbian with a therapist will depend on the client, the client's ethnic or cultural history, the presenting problem, the therapist's personality and the therapeutic approach. In *Counselling – The Deaf Challenge*, Mairian Corker (1994) discusses an American study on identity, which found that 87 per cent of black–deaf people who were questioned about their 'double immersion', identified as black first and deaf second. Those who identified as deaf first were largely from deaf families and residential school background. She suggests that as a result of the focus on black cultural history as opposed to deaf cultural history, many black–deaf people have a reduced emphasis on deafness. It may also be indicative of the complexity by which race is understood within the deaf community in terms of internalized disabilism, sub-cultural racism and projections of 'otherness'. This seems to be evident in all the sub-cultures of the 'other'. For example, Coyle et al. say, 'Research on lesbians and gay men from ethnic minority communities has highlighted the ways in which the particular voices of these groups have been ignored or downplayed within much existing work on lesbian and gay sexualities' (1999: 140–1). There appears to be evidence (at least anecdotally) to suggest that accusations of 'otherness' is levelled against and within these sub groups. For example, the blacks accuse the Jews of being racist; the gay and lesbian community accuse black men of being homophobic, and many others. Such gross generalizations are not only erroneous and dangerous but tend to reinforce the myths of stereotyping, which is often perpetuated by the dominant hegemonic social classes.

In terms of the hierarchy of social and cultural identities, Kearney (1996) argues that class remains the dominant position in relation to gender or race. In *Pushing Against the Wind: The Recognition of Lesbians in Counsellor Training*, Crouan has this to say:

> Highlighting homophobia and heterosexism in counselling training is not meant to imply support for the notion that a hierarchy of oppressive experiences exists, with one group being any more or less deserving of attention and support than another. Indeed, many of the suggestions for making counselling training more relevant and accessible to lesbians could equally be applied to black people, disabled people and other members of oppressed groups. (1996: 36)

Clearly there seems to be no hierarchy of identities when we compare and contrast the ways in which the different disadvantaged groups see themselves. As social and cultural categories race, gender, class, disability and sexual orientation have evolved as important signifiers to differentiate and mark out particular spaces for individuals and groups to assert their social, cultural and political 'rights'. As epistemological tools, these categories have been useful in extending the discussion and debate mainly on the critique of hegemonic masculinities, cultural imperialism, racism, sexism and homophobia. In this respect Marxist–socialist ideas, feminist studies, black consciousness, disability movements and gay and lesbian movements have shifted the debate away from the corridors of intellectual theorization and political platforms to the realities of social policies and its consequences on the personal and psychological lives of people. They have also provided us with the necessary vocabularies to articulate difference critically and not be content with difference as separate and unequal. As Kuper argues,

> Difference multiculturalism is inward looking, self-regarding, pumped up with pride about the importance of a particular culture and its claims to superiority. Critical multiculturalism, in contrast, is outward looking, organized to challenge the cultural prejudices of the dominant social class, intent on uncovering the vulnerable underbelly of the hegemonic discourse (1999: 232).

In counselling in the UK, although these categories are not constructed consciously to divide and sub-divide human beings in any hierarchical way, they can become problematic when perceptions and conceptualizations create ambiguous and confusing responses thus leading counsellors and psychotherapists to be unknowingly essentialist, sometimes falling into the ideological traps of stereotyping negatively. Sashidharan (1986) reminds us that when concepts such as race, culture and ethnicity take on politically loaded meanings, they become powerful tools in the hands of psychiatrists, counsellors and psychotherapists. People's life experiences become reduced to mere manageable problems falling within the clinical competence of the culturally informed practitioner. When this happens culture becomes the site within which the counsellor looks for the clinical problem, and ignores the structural dimensions of contemporary racism, sexism, homophobia. The treatment is then isolated from the day-to-day struggles – racism, sexism, homophobia, disabilism, ageism – of the client (see also Ahmad, 1996; Fernando, 1988; Marks, 1999).

Therapy and therapists' attitudes towards the 'other'

The very little research that has investigated the attitude of counsellors and psychotherapists towards the black, the disabled, the homosexual and the working class seems to indicate that negative reactions are shown to certain of these sub groups. For example, on homosexuality, Hayes & Erkis suggest, 'The combination of client sexual orientation and therapist homophobia has been found to predict negative reactions to homosexual clients' (2000: 17). Although a substantial amount of non-pathologizing literature has been produced on gay and lesbian issues, since the removing of homosexuality as pathological by the American Psychiatric Association from its 'Diagnostic and Statistical Manual' in 1973 (Coyle et al., 1999), the practice of counselling with gay and lesbian clients still appears to be failing in terms of an authentic anti-discriminatory process. The problem, according to Irigaray, lies with some of the earliest writers in this field. For example, in *Speculum of the Other Woman*, Irigaray (1985) critically examines Freud's, Lacan's and other psychoanalytic work for phallocentrism. In a later work, she argues that Freud 'interprets women's suffering, their symptoms, their dissatisfactions, in terms of their individual histories, without questioning the relationship of their "pathology" to a certain state of society, of culture. As a result, he generally ends up resubmitting women to the dominant discourse of the father, to the law of the father, while silencing their demands' (Irigaray, 1991: 119–20). Some of the theories of the other 'founding fathers' [*sic*] have also been critically examined. For example, Dalal (1988) is critical of some of Jung's writing (see also Thomas & Sillen, 1972: 239; Masson, 1988).

In general, however, counselling has been critiqued for being: Eurocentric, ethnocentric, individualistic (see Carter, 1995; Lago & Thompson, 1996; Moodley, 1999; Sashidharan, 1990; Sue & Sue, 1990), middle-class (see Kearney, 1996), generally focusing on heterosexual issues, and in practice for promoting the YAVIS effect (clients who are seen to be or perceived to be young, attractive, verbal, intelligent and single) (see Holmes, 1993; Katz, 1985). Furthermore, as a 'talking-cure' with an emphasis on the analysis of the 'utterances of distress' through the speech act(ion), counselling relegates other cultural forms of communication to the margins, for example, BSL (British Sign Language of the deaf) (see Corker, 1994). Therefore, it seems that counselling practice has been contained by a particular cultural history, a medical objectivity and a clinical subjectivity which on the surface appears to be liberal, flexible and creative but can also be experienced as oppressive for black, working class, disabled, gay and lesbian clients. These clients may sense that they have become the crucible, the containing object, where the heterosexual, middle class, white unconscious is equated with the consciousness of the 'other'. In terms of race and ethnicity, post colonial writers such as Bhabha (1994), Said (1978), Fanon (1952 [1967]) and

Spivak (1988) have also critiqued the negative function of the western European ego which projects on to the 'other', 'the dark continent'[5], its anxieties and tensions. This expression of the western European collective projection is textualized in the pseudo-scientific racism, which informed the theories of mental (ill) health during the 19th century (see Thomas & Sillen, 1972) .

As a way out of this dilemma, counselling has begun to include issues of race, gender, class, disability and sexual orientation in its theory and practice. But each of these inclusions seem to follow a fairly 'straight' and monocultural process, *viz.*, for black and ethnic groups there is cross-cultural or intercultural counselling; for gay men there is gay counselling; for lesbian women there is lesbian therapy; for some women there is feminist therapy; for the deaf person there is deaf counselling, and in this particular way individuals are grouped, stereotyped and marginalized. Each occupies a social, cultural and political space within which the psychological needs of its members are deemed to be met. Or are they met? Undertaking a critical and developmental analysis of the present practice of counselling for each disadvantaged group is essential to the future of counselling.

Comprehending the complexity of multiple identities

In the social and health sciences with the exception of psychiatry, psychotherapy and psychoanalysis, the categories of race, gender, class, disability and sexual orientation appear to be highlighted in research, theory and practice. Counselling appears to fall between these two worlds. On the one hand, with its history of psychotherapy and psychoanalysis, it has tended to avoid or rather emphasize metapsychology and the internal world; while on the other hand, with its roots in education and social sciences, it has always refused to beckon to the call of the unconscious to stay silent about the social and the cultural condition of the client. Yet the only way for counsellors to engage with the categories of race, gender, class, disability and sexual orientation was to separate, isolate and deconstruct them individually so as to contain them therapeutically.

This construction of separate categories has been effective up to a point. The specific labelling of race, gender, class, disability and sexual orientation has allowed each of the oppressed groups to find their own socio-political and psycho-cultural voice within the dominant discourse of therapy. But counselling and therapy is more than a social, cultural or political strategy. For therapy to be organized and delivered primarily around the classification of the 'other' can in the long-term lead to further oppression. For many disadvantaged clients, it seems that when it comes to their pain, discomfort, distress and illness, these tend to disappear in the interpretation and analysis in therapy, and are replaced by the sociology of race, gender, class, disability and sexual orientation. These psycho-cultural identities can initially act as variables within mental (ill) health but eventually construct themselves as the source of the problem. This point is also argued by Fernando, when he says, 'Cultures that are different become cultures that are problematic, pathological, inferior (1988: 155). So, for example, the Asian woman in an arranged marriage, the culture shock of an asylum seeker, the 'coming-out' of the final year student, or the dreadlocks of the rapping Rastafarian can be seen as 'pathological', and counsellors and therapists tend to 'home' in on these issues when the client is understood solely and exclusively within the categories race, gender, class, disability and sexual orientation.

Can therapy in its present state comprehend the complexity of being black, gay, working-class, deaf … ? The answer must be a 'Yes', because as the individual chapters in this volume testify there is a concern by professionals that these issues be addressed in counselling. But what of the client who is black, disabled, homosexual and working class? Can the practice of counselling offer a space for all the voices of this (hypothetical) client? Is the theory sophisticated enough to accommodate the subtle nuances, multiple metaphors and the complex experiencing of a client who chooses to represent all these identities in therapy? If not, then counsellors may find themselves 'hearing multiple voices' and not knowing what to make of it. Their only recourse is to find theoretical security in the psychiatrist's 'fourth bag of diagnostic (hat)tricks' (for example, DSM IV) to pronounce the client as having multiple personality disorder, schizophrenia or any other medicalized identification and label.

For counselling to incorporate both the visible and invisible disadvantages, the external and internal voice, the social and the psychological presentations of 'self', the theory, training and the research in this field must accept the idea of multiple identities and pluralities of the self. At this juncture – innovative research methodology, theoretical epistemologies, practice insights – where the discourse of counselling advances its practice we may find that counsellors can move beyond the singular categories of race, gender, class, disability and sexual orientation to one which incorporates the complexity of all these experiences. For example, a black client would not be offered 'multicultural counselling' but a 'new multi(ple) cultural therapy' which incorporates race, gender, class, disability and sexual orientation.[6] This is a change which Sue (1997) and Lago and Thompson (1996) have called for when they suggested that all counselling should be multicultural and emphasize the need for training therapists to work with issues of race, gender, class, disability, sexual orientation, age, different religious affiliations, etc.

If therapists are to 'work' with, through and beyond their cultural, racial, ethnic, sexual and class differences and offer an authentic anti-oppressive practice, then this must be supported by research, theory and training that is inclusive of all aspects of race, gender, class, disability and sexual orientation. Practitioners must also be aware that they themselves could easily reproduce the oppressive structures that clients are experiencing. Wilson and Beresford, who examined anti-oppressive social work practice, had this to say,

> We have seen little to indicate that proponents acknowledge their *own* political role within the structures and apparatus of the 'anti-oppressive' machine. By this we mean little acknowledgement that anti-oppressive theorists and practitioners may *themselves* be contributing to oppressive constructions and definitions of service users and their problems *however 'anti-oppressively' they claim they are operating'* (2000: 558). [Italics in original]

Therefore reconstituting and redefining the multi(ple) cultural descriptors of counselling may be necessary, although we are aware that emptying out the (multicultural) crucibles may not be entirely possible or desirable for some clients at a particular stage in their therapy. It must be acknowledged that an exclusive focus on issues of race, gender, class, disability and sexual orientation is sometimes inevitable, to allow for 'containing objects' of 'cultural inheritance' (Winnicott, 1971) to surface and find meaning in the client. For example, on issues of race, Janet Helms maintains, 'It is by no means clear that the same competencies required to deliver effective services to clients for whom racial-group membership is central are equally appropriate for clients for whom other social identities (for example, gender, age, or religion) are more central' (1994: 163).

This reconstitution is also encouraged by the British Association for Counselling and Psychotherapy. For example, the requirement for individual accreditation by the BACP states that applicants should be asked to supply evidence that they have addressed the issues of difference and equality in their practice. However, very few counselling training courses offer 'theoretical and clinical skills that prepare trainees to work with ethnic minority clients as well as with "Other" clients from the disabled, gay and lesbian communities' (Moodley, 2000: 154).

Complexity of experiencing and expressing multi(ple) cultural oppressions

Explaining 'illness', discomfort and subjective distress through any of one or more of the 400 therapies that are available (Garfield & Bergin, 1986) has proved to be an effective way in which clients manage many of life's dilemmas, but it has also shown itself to be limited in a number of other ways. For example, the theory of counselling appears to show very little understanding of the complex ways in which clients experience multiple oppressions. It is possible that some clients may express two or more of the social constructions of race, gender, class, disability and sexual orientation when they are in conversation with the therapist. Therapists would need to be aware, and open to the possibility that clients may choose to speak in the voice of ONE or MORE of the multi(ple) cultural 'OTHER'. For example, clients may articulate a very detailed and clear narrative of feelings of oppression and discrimination through the voice of race and ethnicity whilst alluding to scenarios of distress and illness around the theme of gender and sexuality. For the counsellor the difficult task would be to tease out the strands which contextualize gender from race, or gender from ethnicity, and where does the issue of sexuality fit into this model of deconstruction? It not only raises issues about counselling skills and multicultural competencies but it also challenges the counsellor's understanding and awareness of the socio-political complexities of gender, race and ethnicity, especially in a post colonial setting. Not an easy task for the therapist, but one which can make the invisible and the unheard voice, in this case of gender, to be seen, felt and heard in the transference and countertransference processes.

Other clients, for example, may want to discuss issues of race, but find it problematic therapeutically. The client may find it more comfortable or psychologically strategic to use the language, vocabulary, linguistic codes, the epistemologies of gender as a way to engage with the issues of race and ethnicity. This was seen with Mary (not her real name), who was in therapy with a black counsellor and who found it difficult initially to accept her black woman counsellor (see Moodley and Dhingra, 1998 for a complete case study and discussion):

> Mary: When I first realized that you are different race to me. I did think she can't be able to help me you know she, eh, especially, I used to live in, a big Asian community around a big Asian community in (…) and they were so very different to me.

The strategy that Mary adopted in accepting her black counsellor and being able to talk about issues of 'race', culture and ethnicity was to employ the notion, the vocabularies of gender. For example,

> *Mary:* … but I do feel you understand me
> *Counsellor:* Um
> *Mary:* I feel understood as a woman
> *Counsellor:* Um

Mary: When especially a lot of my issues in patriarchal society in and stuff like that and I feel you understand me. I can trust you.

To examine 'race' as a variable in therapy can sometimes create a disturbance or turbulence of the unconscious for the client, or the therapist, or both. In a maturing or becoming relationship, with its sensitive and delicate boundaries, the process of counselling may not be able to contain the contradictions and paradoxes which a discussion on race may bring. So the 'safe' way to engage in therapy for this client is to speak from 'outside' the preconceived ideas and notions of race in counselling, but 'inside' the culture of gender. Race then becomes more acceptable because gender provides it with a particular set of vocabularies, epistemologies and linguistic resonance which can be 'held' in the Winnocottian sense. This 'holding environment' gives both client and therapist time to come together to a point of knowing that it will be 'safe' to discuss the questions, issues and traumas, in this case of race, but the same could be applied to gender, class, disability and sexual orientation.

Working in this way would allow for the multiple layers of a client's 'self' to be privileged over the stereotyped, transhistorical and bio-medical model which appears to be the norm in counselling. Therefore, to explore the interconnections between and amongst these various forms of discriminations and oppressions in counselling with the 'other' client, counsellors must not only be multicompetent in the areas of race, gender, class, disability and sexual orientation, but also, and more importantly, to examine some of their deep-seated prejudices and biases, which is not easy or comfortable to do.

Conclusion

In counselling, if any *one* of the client's multiple voices happens to be denied or repressed then it seems that the client is experiencing double, triple or multi(ple) cultural jeopardy. For the counsellor working in this way may appear to be problematic or even pathological. It may even test to the limits some of the ideas that govern 'interpreting the transference', and may also create uncomfortable and sometimes unacceptable counter-transference feelings, in the therapist.

In therapy the meaning-making or the (re)construction of therapeutic narratives are dependent on both parties not only accepting and acknowledging each other's differences and similarities in terms of gender, class, ethnicity, disability or sexual orientation but to conduct therapy in a human rights framework within which the client's individual and very personal multi(ple) cultural rights and rites are understood and respected. So when a therapist is 'working with' a deaf client who also happens to be black, gay and working class, counselling will need to reflect these various multiple cultural identities to claim the hallowed ground of anti-oppressive practice.

Notes

1 'Race' is is understood not as a biologically determined concept but as a product of specific social and political histories.

2 Race, gender, class, disability, sexual orientations are understood in a post-structuralist way as processes which are not defined by biological determinism, or any psycho-social essentialism, nor any *a priori* notions of the 'self'. These 'other' voices and the cultures and identities that they represent are seen as dynamic processes constantly changing and reinventing themselves, fragmenting and unifying, and reforming and transforming themselves, within different spaces and different times in complex and contesting ways. Depending on how these ideas are produced and reproduced within society, it can offer the temptation to generalize a universality about the disadvantaged client on the basis of common humanity or it can form the basis of constructing the notion of 'difference' as a symbiotic and mutually creative 'other'.

3 The two major philosophies that theorize the problematic of the 'other', are discussed by Theunissen (1977). The 'other' is defined as the difference between the 'thou' (as the 'second person' of the personal pronoun, the one who is addressed, the partner of discourse or of 'dialogue', a process known as 'dialogicalism'), and the alien I (the alter-ego or being-with-the-other, a process known as 'transcendentalism'). Theunissen's very detailed investigation into the philosophy of Husserl, Heidegger, Satre and Buber shows a complex theoretical and philosophical understanding on the problem of the 'other'. These concepts which have been the foundations of post-enlightenment thinking on social thought and practice have provided the historical and theoretical framework from which Freud, Jung, Lacan and others in the counselling and psychotherapy world have understood the problematic of the 'other', intersubjectivity and the development of the Ego.

4 The projection of negative aspects of one's self onto the 'other' is known as otherness. It could be understood as a fragmentation and splitting of the 'self', reflecting a lack of integration of 'self' during the earlier period of the individual. Objects were then found outside oneself on which to project this split of part of the 'self' (one's shadow or repressed material). Starting from the *mother* being the first 'other', the baby projects its anxieties outside itself, as a defence. But as part of development the infant needs to integrate this split-off self as a part of individuation (Benvenuto & Kennedy, 1986). The inability to undergo this integration leads to 'primal repression and as such it returns into the unconscious' (Lemaire, 1970: 115) from where it will eventually be projected as the 'bad internal objects' (Klein, 1921: 45) onto the 'other' because the 'other' is the locus in which the 'I' is constituted symbolically.

Different crucibles were found through the centuries to project the negative internalized objects, viz., race, gender, class, disability, religious and sexual orientation. For example, women who challenged hegemonic patriarchy and who attempted to communicate their inner reality were trapped in the 'gaze' of a society which incarcerated or burnt them at the stake, as a defence against deep negative anxieties which surfaced through collective ego identification. These 'witches or folk devils' became the represented image of an aspect of the internal negative object. This objectification of women, in later centuries like the Victorian period, manifested itself in the representation of working class women as sexual objects. Similarly, mental and physical disability and in more recent times homosexuality appear to have become the receptacles for much negative projection.

5 Freud (1926) wrote, 'The sexual life of adult women is a dark continent' (p. 212). He claimed that the unconscious of the west is equated to the consciousness of black people, the dark continent (see Moodley, 1999; Lago & Moodley, 2000).

6 Many writers have been critical of the 'old' multicultural counselling, for example, Pedersen and Ivey (1994) criticize the narrow 'multiethnic' definition of multiculturalism.

References

Ahmad, W.I.U. (1996) 'The Trouble with Culture', in D. Kelleher & S. Hillier (eds), *Researching Cultural Differences in Health*. London: Routledge.

Benvenuto, B. & Kennedy, R. (1986) *The Works of Jacques Lacan: An Introduction*. London: Free Association Books.

Bhabha, H. (1994) *The Location of Culture*. London: Routledge.

Blakemore, K. & Boneham, M. (1994) *Age, Race and Ethnicity: A Comparative Approach*. Buckingham: Open University Press.

Carter, R.T. (1995) *The Influence of Race and Racial Identity in Psychotherapy*. New York: Wiley.

Corker, M. (1994) *Counselling – The Deaf Challenge*. London: Jessica Kingsley Publishers.

Coyle, A., Milton, M. & Annesley, P. (1999) 'The Silencing of Lesbian and Gay Voices in Psychotherapeutic Texts and Training', *Changes, International Journal of Psychology and Psychotherapy*, 17(2), pp. 132–43.

Crouan, M. (1996) 'Pushing Against the Wind: The Recognition of Lesbians in Counselling Training', *Counselling, Journal of the British Association for Counselling*, 7(1), pp. 36–9.

Dalal, F. (1988) 'Jung, a Racist', *British Journal of Psychotherapy*, 4, pp. 263–79.

Fanon, F. (1952) *Black Skin, White Masks*. New York: Grove Press.

Fernando, S. (1988) *Race and Culture in Psychiatry*. Kent: Croom Helm.

Freud, S. (1926) *The Question of Lay Analysis: Conversations with an Impartial Person*. (Standard Edition, 20), pp. 183–258. London: Hogarth Press.

Garfield, S.L. & Bergin, A. (eds) (1986) *Handbook of Psychotherapy and Behavior Change*. New York: Wiley.

Hayes, J.A. & Erkis, A.J. (2000) 'Therapist Homophobia, Client Sexual Orientation, and Source of Client HIV Infection as Predicators of Therapist Reactions to Clients With HIV', *Journal of Counseling Psychology*, 47(1), pp. 71–8.

Helms, J.E. (1994) 'How Multiculturalism Obscures Racial Factors in the Therapy Process: Comment on Ridley et al. (1994), Sodowsky et al. (1994), Ottavi et al. (1994), and Thompson et al. (1994)', *Journal of Counseling Psychology*, 41: pp. 162–5.

Holmes, J. (1993) *Between Art and Science: Essays in Psychotherapy and Psychiatry*. London: Routledge.

Irigaray, L. (1985) *Speculum of the Other Woman*, trans. G.C. Gill. Ithaca, NY: Cornell University.

Irigaray, L. (1991) *The Irigaray Reader*. Oxford: Blackwell.

Jenness, L. (1972) *Feminism and Socialism*. New York: Pathfinder Press.

Katz, J.H. (1985) 'The Sociopolitical Nature of Counselling', *The Counseling Psychologist*, 13(4), pp. 615–25.

Kearney, A. (1996) *Counselling, Class and Politics: Undeclared Influences in Therapy*. Ross-on-Wye: PCCS Books.

Klein, M. (1921–45) (1975) *Love, Guilt, and Reparation and Other Works, 1921–45*. New York: Free Press.

Kuper, A. (1999) *Culture*. Cambridge, MA: Harvard University Press.

Lago, C. & Thompson, J. (1996) *Race, Culture and Counselling*. Buckingham: Open University Press.

Lago, C. & Moodley, R. (2000) 'Multicultural Issues in Integrative and Eclectic Counselling and Psychotherapy', in S. Palmer & R. Woolfe (eds), *Integrative and Eclectic Counselling and Psychotherapy Handbook*. London: Sage.

Lemaire, A. (1970) (1977) *Jacques Lacan*, trans. David Macey. London: Routledge & Kegan Paul.

Lorde, A. (1984) *Sister Outside: Essays and Speeches*. Tramansburg, NY: Crossing Press.

Luthar, S.S., Cushing, G., Merikangas, K.R. & Rounsaville, B.J. (1998) 'Multiple Jeopardy: Risk and Protective Factors among Addicted Mothers' Offspring,' *Journal of Development and Psychopathology*, 10(1), pp. 117–36.

Marks, D. (1999) *Disability: Controversial Debates and Psychosocial Perspectives.* London: Routledge.

Masson, J. (1988) *Against Therapy: Emotional Tyranny and the Myth of Psychological Healing*, Glasgow: Collins.

Moodley, R. (1999) 'Challenges and Transformations: Counselling in a Multicultural Context,' *International Journal for the Advancement of Counselling*, 21(2), pp. 139–52

Moodley, R. (2000) 'Counselling and Psychotherapy in a Multicultural Context: Some Training Issues, Part 1', *Counselling, Journal of the British Association for Counselling*, 11, pp. 154–57.

Moodley, R. & Dhingra, S. (1998) 'Cross-Cultural/Racial Matching in Counselling and Therapy: White Clients and Black Counsellors,' *Counselling, Journal of the British Association for Counselling*, 9, pp. 295–99.

Norman, A. (1985) *Triple Jeopardy: Growing Old in a Second Homeland*. London: Centre for Policy on Ageing.

Paz, J. & Aleman, S. (1998) 'The Yaqui Elderly of Old Pascua', *Journal of Gerontological Social Work*, 30(1–2), pp. 47–59.

Pedersen, P. & Ivey, A.E. (1994) *Culture-centred Counseling and Interviewing Skills*. Westpoint, CT: Greenwood/Praeger.

Said, E.W. (1978) *Orientalism*. London: Routledge & Kegan Paul.

Sashidharan, S. (1986) 'Ideology and Politics in Transcultural Psychiatry', in J.L. Cox, (ed.), *Transcultural Psychiatry*. London: Croom Helm.

Sashidharan, S. (1990) 'Race and Psychiatry', *Medical World*, 3, pp. 8–12.

Spivak, G.C. (1988) *In Other Worlds*. London: Routledge.

Sue, D. (1997) 'Multicultural Training', *International Journal of International Relations*, 21, pp. 175–93.

Sue, D.W. & Sue, D. (1990) *Counseling the Culturally Different: Theory and Practice*. New York: John Wiley & Sons.

Theunissen, M. (1997) (1984) *The Other*, trans. C. Macann. Boston, MA: Massachusetts Institute of Technology.

Thomas, A. & Sillen, S. (1972) *Racism and Psychiatry*. Secaucus, NJ: Citadel.

Wilson, A. & Beresford, P. (2000) 'Anti-Oppressive Practice: Emancipation or Appropriation?', *British Journal of Social Work*, 39(5), pp. 555–73.

Winnicott, D.W. (1971) *Playing and Reality*. London: Tavisock Publications.

11 *Oppression and Pedagogy: Anti-oppressive Practice in the Education of Therapists*

Barbara Smith and Keith Tudor

In recent years there has been a growing awareness that traditional training for counsellors and psychotherapists fails to embrace the needs of oppressed and marginalized groups. Ridley suggests that practitioners qualifying from such training courses 'should come to terms with the inadequacy of their preparation for service delivery' (1995: 11) – and goes as far as saying that in some respects their training constitutes a liability for their clients. Despite a rich history of radicalism in the field of psychotherapy, many therapists (we use the term generically to include psychotherapists, counsellors and counselling psychologists) appear politically naive: 'they [therapists] come through professional education which gives them little understanding of social and political issues ... they are ignorant of their place in society ... they are victims of a narrow horizon' (Glen, 1971: 14). It is as if psyche has become separated from society. Research undertaken by Smith into the attitudes of student counsellors towards marginalized groups highlights a worrying lack of political awareness on the part of individual students matched by a lack of adequate emphasis on their training courses on the relevance and impact of oppression, discrimination, marginalization and power. Statements such as 'I can't be racist, my daughter's boyfriend is black – but he's got a chip on his shoulder' and 'I'd be fine working with gay people as a counsellor, but I wouldn't want to have one as a friend' were among the more oppressive responses pointed up by this research (Smith, 1996). While some therapists may be ignorant, others are not happy with this state of affairs. In a study of qualified counsellors conducted by Bimrose and Bayne (1995), 89 per cent reported feelings of discomfort or difficulty when dealing with client 'difference' – 'discomfort' being defined as anxiety, disquiet, confusion, embarrassment, unease and irritation.

This personal naivety and discomfort has deep roots in the history and organization of therapy. Psychoanalysis, psychotherapy and, more recently, counselling have (severally and as one) been consistently criticized for their conservatism and conformity, their uncritical acceptance of oppressive social mores and norms, and, in some instances, their positive advocacy of social (re)adjustment. Examples include:

- The submission/agreement of the International Psychoanalytic Association in the early 1930s to exclude Jewish psychoanalysts from the Berlin Psychoanalytic Institute (see Cocks, 1997).
- The participation of psychoanalysts in the US Appeals of Communism Project in the 1950s, to which a number of therapists provided case studies of their Communist patients, thereby not only breaching patient confidentiality but also acting as political informers (see Schwartz, 1999).
- The oppression of gay therapists especially by the psychoanalytic establishment through the pathologizing of homosexuality (see, for example, O'Connor & Ryan, 1993). To this day, the Association for Christian Counsellors supports counsellors who seek to 'turn' their gay male and lesbian clients back to heterosexuality.

We take the title for this chapter from the inspiring book *Pedagogy of the Oppressed* by Paulo Freire (1972), the Brazilian educationalist, who developed a method of teaching literacy amongst the oppressed which became a means for social change – and who was subsequently imprisoned and exiled for his pains. Although it has accrued a slightly pejorative tone, 'pedagogy' means the practice of teaching. As there is no such thing as a *neutral* educational process (all processes are value-based), our interest in this chapter is to examine the educational practice and process of training therapists, specifically regarding issues of oppression and working with oppressed groups. Although our focus is on education (and training), we consider the implications of these discussions as equally applicable to the ongoing professional and personal development of therapists, through supervision, continuing professional development and personal therapy. Following a brief discussion of oppression and anti-oppressive practice in training, we outline a number of themes in the education of therapists which, in our view, promote anti-oppressive practice in the learning environment, each of which have practical implications for the education/ training of therapists more attuned to the nuances of oppression as expressed in and indeed through the therapeutic milieu.

Anti-oppressive practice in training

Over the years there has been considerable debate about the nature and value of what was (and sometimes still is) called equal opportunities training (EOT). The various terms used – multi-cultural education, race awareness training (RAT), anti-racist training (ART) and, most recently, anti-oppressive practice (AOP) – all represent different and differing approaches to the subject and the process of 'training' or education – and all have been roundly criticized (see, for example, Gurnah, 1984; Sivanandan, 1985; Wilson & Beresford, 2000).

Some of these 'awareness' training courses – often imposed (through compulsory attendance) on a captive, reluctant, defensive and hostile audience – not only determine the content of the course, but also promote one (right) way of 'teaching' and 'being aware' over more student- or participant-centred, facilitated learning. The guilt that this kind of training induces at a personal, collective and institutional level led to one black colleague not being re-employed as a trainer for a particular Local Authority Social Services Department after complaints from the white participants on one course that he had not been hard enough on them!

Some training seeks to raise awareness through experiencing. Disability awareness training (DAT), comprising exercises which simulate blindness, deafness and mobility impairment by using blindfolds, wheelchairs, etc., may be well-intentioned and may even offer some insight into the needs of disabled people, but are ultimately limited and can be deeply offensive. French (1996) criticizes the use of such simulation exercises which ultimately serve to contribute to, rather than challenge, damaging stereotypes. Wood (1990), for instance, describes how 'non-disabled' children using wheelchairs and splints to simulate impairment later reported that they would feel unhappy, sad and lonely if they were disabled, thus adding to a 'tragedy model' of disability and the individualization of impairment.

Nor have liberal therapeutic notions of the person and their behaviour helped anti-oppressive practice. The notion of a balanced individual and a society in stasis and at ease with itself has found succour in the humanistic and therapeutic mantra: 'Criticize the behaviour, not the person'. While this may have made it easier for people to accept and offer tentative criticism, it depersonalizes oppression, reducing it to a 'bad' (or 'mad') behaviour, rather than being the subject of a more thorough, critical, personal and social/political analysis. One of the challenges of Carl Rogers' work and specifically his theory of personality (Rogers, 1951) is that behaviour *is* the person.

Each theoretical approach in therapy has its own (implicit or explicit) notions about power; and, indeed, the notion of power itself and its impact on the therapeutic relationship – let alone the training relationship – is addressed more or less in different approaches. We find the emphasis in the person-centred approach on personal power (see Rogers, 1978) particularly useful, that is: 'the ability to act effectively under one's own volition rather than under external control. It is a state wherein the individual is aware of and can act upon his or her own feelings, needs, and values rather than looking to others for direction' (Natiello, 1987: 210). Natiello (1990) goes on to describe an equality of power in relationship, describing co-operative or 'collaborative power' as characterized by:

1 Openness (all information is fully shared).
2 Responsiveness (all needs and ideas are carefully heard).
3 Dignity (everyone is respected and considered).
4 Personal empowerment (each person has both freedom and responsibility to participate fully).
5 Alternating influence (the impact on process is shared).
6 Co-operation rather than competition.

This in effect defines or describes a pedagogy of equality.

Ultimately, it is not difference – colour, gender, physical or mental impairment, class or sexuality – that is a problem. The problem is that difference is made a problem. A friend of one of the authors once said: 'There's no difference between you and me. The difference is that those stairs segregate me from you.' Thus anti-oppressive practice must account for the *structural* differences – poverty as a result of economic and political systems, discrimation as a result of particular social policies, segregation through a disabling environment, etc. – all of which create and perpetuate divisions and make a problem of difference.

In order to counteract the problem of difference and, furthermore, to promote a positive and cooperative (rather than competitive) learning environment in which both structural (social/political/economic) issues as well as professional and personal issues may be identified and addressed, the rest of this chapter discusses a number of themes which, in our view and based on experience and study, frame anti-oppressive practice in the education of therapists.

The centrality of exploitation to oppression

It is perhaps (hopefully) a commonplace to define oppression as discrimination plus power, that is, a distinction or differentiation made between people which is backed up *and exploited* by a difference of power between the two parties. We emphasize the element of exploitation as it is precisely this 'turning to account' which gives an active sense to oppression, as distinct from it being a passive state. In this sense, the term 'oppression' is thrown around too often and too loosely. It has become a fashionable although crude psychological stick with which to beat others. It is as if it is enough to say 'I *feel* oppressed' to evoke guilt and shame – which is perhaps not surprising in a current social and political culture which positively promotes naming and shaming. This is not to deny the reality of oppression and feelings of oppression or to turn these back onto the subject, claiming that they have a chip on their shoulder; it is to be clear about the distinct elements of discrimination, power *and* exploitation. Thus, in our view, the key to a more precise and useful understanding of oppression in practice and in training is an understanding of individualism, competition and exploitation: 'in capitalist society, the leading ideological edge of Internalised Oppression is *individualism* – the set of beliefs which places the individual above the collective. Behaviour inspired by individualism takes a certain form as well, and that form is *competition*' (Costello, Roy & Steiner, 1988: 55).

In terms of moral philosophy and ethical and professional practice, 'non exploitation' may be viewed as a part of the practitioner's commitment to 'non maleficence' or doing no harm. Rather than simply defining something as oppressive, the principle of non-exploitation invites – indeed challenges – people to think about the therapeutic relationship (see, for instance, Tudor, 1999) and the pedagogic/educational (teacher/student) relationship. It is easy to condemn a trainer having a relationship with a student as necessarily oppressive. It is both more complex and perhaps more human *and* more demanding to subject such a relationship to analysis and understanding in terms of whether it is discriminatory (debatable), whether it involves a power relationship (certainly), and whether it is exploitative (questionable). Again, we do not condone or defend such relationships; we seek to raise these points in the search for greater understanding and clarity.

Practical considerations

Much of the work here is concerned with raising awareness or consciousness – or *conscientizaçao* – a term, originally coined by Freire (which translates as conscientization). This refers to learning to perceive social, political and economic contradictions and, consequently, to take action against the oppressive elements of society. An important part of this is eliciting, challenging and giving feedback to students about the more subtle nuances of oppression in tone and gesture as well as the more obvious oppressive language in speech.

Thompson refers to the 'dangers' in this work: 'anti-discriminatory practice challenges people's values and their taken-for-granted assumptions in constructing their own sense of reality. Such challenges can prove to be very threatening and destabilising' (1997: 159). The subsequent backlash for trainers can also be difficult if they are not clear about their position or sensitive towards those with whom they are working. Holding the existential life position 'I'm OK, You're OK' is essential in challenging and being challenged. Thompson (1998) advises 'elegant challenging' which includes: being tactful and constructive; avoiding cornering people, and allowing them to save face; and that such challenging be undertaken in a spirit of genuine compassion and a commitment to social justice (rather than one of taking the moral high ground). Reflexive discussion and debate are a necessary part of this process. However, these discussions can evoke strong feelings of anger, shame, guilt and grief, and our ability as trainers to manage the intrapsychic and interpersonal consequences is crucial. Mutual and peer support; good, reflective supervision; further training and consultation, where appropriate: are all, in our view, necessary conditions for the maintenance of counselling trainers.

The relevance of the different levels of oppression

Jones (1972) identifies four levels in which (originally) racism is expressed: personal, interpersonal, institutional and cultural – and, in its typical expression, all four levels interact. Thus, in addition to its multiple construction in terms of identity (see Chapter 10), oppression may also be understood on a number of levels. We find this helpful in accounting for (rather than discounting) the dynamics of oppression, especially in the interpersonal field.

It is all too common for a student to operate from a position of internalized oppression (personal level) – and for a trainer either to reinforce this through transactions which in effect pathologize the student, or, conversely, to take the blame and feel bad. While both strategies are also personal, the trainer may also be reflecting and perpetuating an institutional level of oppression. It is often easier to 'blame' institutional forms of oppression 'out there', especially in (or in relation to) institutions in (or with) which we, as trainers feel powerless. It is perhaps less easy to acknowledge the interpersonal dynamics whereby oppression is perpetuated and for the trainer to consider what part they play in furthering an oppressive dynamic and culture, for instance, through their own uncritical acceptance of institutional norms, or through promoting a personality cult centring on the trainer/guru (for a critique of which, see Robertson, 1993).

Practical considerations

Courses are predominantly populated by white, middle class students. If courses want to change this profile, consideration should be given to where and how to advertise and to distribute publicity material. Direct contact with black, gay and disability organizations can be helpful in assuring a wider representation of society on the course and, ultimately, in the counselling/psychotherapy profession. Publicity material should include the course's (and course staff's) commitment to anti-oppressive practice or some equivalent statement outlining the course philosophy in this respect (institutional/cultural levels).

Courses and staff need to have the confidence and support to work through issues of oppression, discrimination, exploitation, etc. in the interpersonal field, i.e. between students, between staff and students, and between staff (interpersonal).

Similarly, but perhaps most sensitively, courses and staff can ultimately only serve the students if they can help each and every student understand their own internal dynamics and processes in relation to oppression. Again, according to different approaches to therapy, this will be understood in different terms – and will also be the subject of the student's personal therapy as well as their professional development on the course.

The impact of different theories concerning the person and behaviour

This is concerned both with the theories espoused by courses regarding personality and behaviour and the (parallel) understanding of the 'behaviour' of the student – which also relate to theories about power. If you believe that *'behaviour is basically the goal-directed attempt of the organism to satisfy its needs as experienced, in the field as perceived'* (Rogers, 1951: 491, original italics), then a different range of responses follow than those implied by a separation of behaviour from the person. In our experience in practice, this requires a lot of patience and willingness to engage in *process* with regard both to the individual student and to the learning group, as well as an attitude and practice on the part of the staff of being open to criticism. This contrasts with approaches to teaching, primarily based on models of child development, which infantilize the adult learner through: (i) making assumptions about their ability to access and process knowledge ('They're not ready for that yet'), and/or (ii) discounting their previous and/or current experience outside the course, for instance, as a trainer in their own right in another field.

Of course we need to be aware of the broader cultural context of theories of therapy and to explore different theories and different ways of reaching a wide(r) range of students and clients. Taylor-Muhammad tells of her struggle with racism throughout her own counsellor training and, in referring specifically to the theories of Freud, Jung and others about dreams and symbols as 'gateways' between unconscious and conscious worlds, writes: 'I honour the fact that these men believed in themselves enough to offer their ideas to the world at the same time that I propose offering recognition and consideration of theorists of African and Asian heritage'. She herself offers training specifically for black counsellors where the work of black theorists is explored – and which also endorses 'gateways' as 'connecting inner and outer, earth and spirit, conscious and unconscious existences' (2001: 11).

Practical considerations
We identify two principal practical considerations to follow from these ideas. One concerns a broader issue of the selection of theories, and the second concerns the selection of students/trainees.

The critique of counselling and psychotherapy as a white, middle class profession is well-made; the parallel criticism that its theoretical base is also predominantly white, western and middle class is also well-substantiated. In an intellectual era of postmodernism, it is in our view incumbent on trainers not only to be drawing on new sources of materials and revisiting and reconstructing old roots, but also to be bringing their critical consciousness to bear on the very foundations and assumptions of therapy such as dual relationships, the nature and purpose of confidentiality, etc.

As far as the selection of trainees is concerned, Wheeler describes this as 'the most crucial phase of assessment (1996: 27). She surveyed counsellor training courses asking respondents to list six criteria they considered to be most important in selecting students. The criteria were grouped under 17 different headings from the lists of forty respondents. The highest number of responses was under the heading 'Qualifications/degree/ability to cope with academic content/ability to translate experience into the written word' with 27 respondents, and the lowest 'Evidence of awareness of minority issues' with only 1 respondent. (This scored lower than 'Financial/time/resources to meet costs' with 3 respondents.) What dangers lurk in the selection process of counselling courses in the face of such evidence? Perhaps we need to re-examine our values and intentions as trainers. What are our criteria for selection? Do they discriminate against people who have already been failed by the education system through institutionalized racism, sexism, etc.? Do they exclude people who have limited finances (see Kearney, 1996). At the interview of one black male candidate, it seemed likely that he would struggle with the academic level of the course. Here was a tall, black, gentle man, flying in the face of media stereotypes, with a wealth of personal experience of surviving racism and a good heart. He was intelligent, warm and genuine. Had the interviewers stayed rigidly with the (academic) selection criteria, a good human being would possibly have been lost to therapy. Of course, this example raises the question of whether counselling and psychotherapy programmes should have an integral academic component – or not. Our preference is that the academic strand should be optional. Perhaps a more profound and challenging question is whether such courses should be located within academic institutions at all.

The importance of the integration of theory and practice

This refers to the desirability, even necessity, of the integration of theory and practice specifically as regards 'difference' and oppression. Apart from the considerable literature on integrative therapy over the past 20 years or so, there is a more personal point as to how (and indeed whether) the practitioner integrates theory, and especially their chosen theoretical orientation, into their practice.

It is important not only that such issues as difference, culture, discrimination, oppression, exploitation, etc. are on the syllabus (however that is determined and/or negotiated), but also that these issues are integrated personally. As Rogers put it, over 50 years ago:

it seems desirable that the student should have a broad experiential knowledge of the human being in his social setting. This may be given, to some extent, by reading or course work in cultural anthropology or sociology. Such knowledge needs to be supplemented by experiences of living with or dealing with individuals who have been the product of cultural influences very different from those which have moulded the student. Such experiences and knowledge often seem necessary to make possible the deep understanding of another (1951: 437).

Such deep experiential learning enhances empathy – which is a good argument for the necessity and efficacy of theory. Furthermore, we argue (along with Rogers) that the student should have a broad experiential knowledge *of themselves* and their social setting. Dalrymple and Burke are clear about the personal and political effect of such experiences: 'individuals who make the connections between their personal condition and the society in which they exist begin to make changes within themselves, within their families and community and wider social structures' (1995: 12). Taking this further, Samuels (2001) tells of a client, an Italian banker, who had a dream about 'a beautiful mountain lake with deep, clear, crystalline water' (5). The client's association with the image was that the lake symbolized his soul or at least his potential 'to develop a deep, clear, soulful attitude to life' (5). His next association related to polluted coastal waters in the Adriatic. He questioned: 'Can one's soul remain pure whilst there is pollution in one's home waters?' (5). The client subsequently went on to give up banking and become active in Green politics in Italy.

Practical considerations

If courses are to take positive action in recruiting students representative of wider society, then it is crucial that support systems are in place, including a readiness on the part of the trainers to address issues as they emerge in the group. How safe is it for example, for a gay, lesbian or bisexual student to 'come out' on this course? How will the staff team deal with other students' homophobia, however subtly expressed? In others words, how 'integrated' are all the students with the course – and how integrated and integrative is the course in its social setting? A colleague describes her experience on her first day of a Postgraduate Diploma in Counselling course where students were paired off to talk to each other about themselves, and then introduce each other to the large group. She told her fellow student of her sexuality and her co-parenting of her daughter with her lesbian partner. The other student did not disclose any of this information to the large group, keeping to 'safe' subjects like 'she has two cats'! Two other lesbians had exactly the same experience in the exercise. We can only guess at the reasons for this phenomenon (fear, shame, homophobia?), but it clearly indicates a need for trainers to discuss openly issues of identity, including sexuality, in constructive and affirming ways. Of course, these issues are crucial not only for the students but also for potential future clients, especially if they go unacknowledged and unchallenged.

It is fair to say that many course providers are working to address issues of anti-oppressive practice, bringing in specialist trainers and offering modules on a variety of issues. While this is to be welcomed, it is essential to offer an integrated training where the issues are raised on an ongoing basis by the regular course team. Practice, case study material, role-play, and discussion of ethical and professional dilemmas – all offer opportunities to explore issues of difference as part of an integrated training. Books other than textbooks can supplement course texts and video material can highlight issues in context: Alice Walker's *The Color Purple* about the oppression of black women, and the film *Philadelphia* about attitudes to AIDS – both raise important issues, whilst at the same time offering opportunities to critique media representations of marginalized groups. Other opportunities are presented through course requirements such as written assignments and presentations. If, for instance, students are researching a topic such as childhood sexual abuse or 'domestic' violence, one of the assessment criteria could be the demonstration of awareness of connections between individual and institutional sexism and these phenomena. Furthermore, in using or referring to case study material, students could evaluate the client's situation in the context of their cultural biography and social situation i.e. 'Is this client's depression due to the daily onslaught of racist psychological and physical abuse?'

The significance of the learning environment

From our frame of reference, it is important to encourage and facilitate 'cooperative social environments' [which] are an ideal ecology for the development of emotional literacy (Steiner, 1984: 167) – and for the development of personal power (Rogers, 1978). Such learning environments need to provide the physical, psychological, conceptual and cultural space set aside for the development of the adult learner. A number of points follow from this:

- That the physical environment is as accessible as possible to all, is aesthetically pleasing, and facilitative of the learning process.

- That both student and trainer are open to learning, to challenging and to being challenged. This avoids the problems commonly associated with narcissistic trainers.
- That the emphasis in learning is on freedom and equality of intellect and expression. This avoids the dangers of conservatism and conformity.
- That systems within the learning organization are transparent and accessible. This promotes democracy and avoids the worst excesses of closed, incestuous systems – for a description of which, see Robertson (1993). It has always seemed a nonsense to us that, for instance, person-centred counselling courses (and recognized and validated ones at that) operate without student organization and representation.
- That the content and process of learning are congruent with the theoretical orientation. It would be somewhat incongruent, for instance, to 'teach' about oppression by means of a didactic presentation. If the message is liberation, then this needs to be reflected in the methodology of the pedagogy (hence the pedagogy of the oppressed) – see Wilson and Beresford (2000) for a critique of the appropriation of users' experience by 'anti-oppressive' academics and for a view of emancipatory research methodology.

A modest example of the facilitation and opening up of the learning environment itself involved a visiting trainer who in working with a group at a training institute generally sat *in* the group rather than 'at the front'. In the feedback at the end of the weekend, one trainee commented that he had never experienced a weekend on which the participants themselves had used the whiteboard so much.

Practical considerations

Ideally, the training agency or institution is committed to offering a facilitative and supportive environment for staff and students to work and learn in, and to implementing policies concerning the recruitment of a diverse staff group and on equal opportunities.

There is a danger that some students are treated as 'experts' in class, race or same sexuality by trainers or the student group, or that they become the focus of attention when discussing issues of culture or racism. Corker (1994), a deaf counsellor, researcher and author, describes some of her experiences on her Diploma course where she felt that there was pressure on her to educate and inform the course on deaf issues. While disclosure of personal experience can be very valuable to the group – and often helpful for the individual in gaining recognition from the group for her/his identity and strength in dealing with oppression – trainers need to check that individuals are comfortable with this attention and to give them strong support, for instance, by challenging other students and colleagues in their own right.

Alexander (2001), a counsellor, trainer and author, writes of her experience as a deaf person trying to access counsellor training and being met with rejection. She highlights the experiences of other deaf and disabled students whose experience of training was one of struggle, both in practical ways and in feeling isolated and unsupported, with lowered levels of confidence and self-esteem. She suggests that this sense of isolation makes it difficult for disabled students to seek the required practical support from the trainers, the group or the college. There are a number of ways and strategies in which 'support' may be offered and accepted. Cropper and Burke highlight the value of using mentors to support students:

> mentoring can be used as part of an anti-oppressive/anti-racist strategy, informed [in this case] by black feminist perspectives, when it can support students who are different, and assist them maintain their sense of self whilst negotiating and developing survival techniques within a multicultural context (2000: 35).

Whilst students may be well supported (supervised and trained) by trainers and tutors across cultural differences (black student/white trainer, etc) – and we do not believe in crude assumptions about 'matching' along lines of race, gender, sexuality, etc. – ideally students should have access to a range of people and support. Having a multiplicity of relationships and experiences across such 'divides' enhances a genuine multiculturalism both structurally and internally. Of course, such support must extend to placements. While we can work at developing our own anti-oppressive practice as trainers, often we do not know the level or kind of support being offered by placement providers. One black student with an Afro-Caribbean accent experienced a high rate of non-attendance by clients after his initial referral conversations (over the phone). This 'drop-out' rate was disproportionate to that amongst the other counselling students within the service. Clearly, this student needed support and encouragement, possibly from a black mentor or supervisor who may have had similar experiences during their training and who could suggest 'survival' strategies. Similarly, gay and lesbian students may be vulnerable to homophobia from some colleagues and/or clients in some placements and course providers need to ensure that agencies offer a protective and supportive environment for students to undertake their practice. Does the agency make explicit their commitment to anti-oppressive practice? How would it support a student who had been hurt by racist/disablist/ homophobic attitudes or behaviours? What pro-active measures are in place to avoid such situations?

Conclusion

In the context of current debates about race and culture – at the time of writing, after the British General Election, June 2001 and against the backdrop of clashes between white and Asian youths in Bradford and Oldham in the summer; the bombing of Afghanistan, after 11 September; and the build up of political tension in the Middle East and between India and Pakistan, December 2001/January 2002 – it is interesting to reflect on the use of language, how language changes, and who decides what may be said. In one televized debate following 11 September between two studio audiences in Islamabad and New York it was clear that there was a distinct lack of empathy, especially from the American audience, about the history and *context* of people's experience in Pakistan and, more broadly, the Muslim world. Much of the so-called debate about race in Britain has focused on who can say what about whom – and thus, in our view, has become diverted into issues of procedure, censorship and political correctness, at the expense of open and honest debates about race, culture, identity, nationality, immigration at both a structural, political level as well as acknowledging the powerful feelings all these issues engender. We hope that some of the points raised in this chapter open up debates concerning learning and oppression and specifically how therapists – and emerging therapists – can best serve their clients in becoming liberated.

Summary

- Therapists need to develop a critical consciousness with regard to oppression in all its forms.
- Exploitation is central to an understanding of oppression.
- There are different constructions and levels of oppression.
- Different theories regarding the person and behaviour – and power – impact on our understanding of oppression.
- The integration of theory and practice on training courses is both desirable and necessary.

- The learning environment is highly significant in promoting (or demoting) open discussion about oppression.
- Specific practical considerations for the training of therapists include support for trainers, the placement of pre-course publicity, the nature of assessment procedures, and ongoing support on the course.

References

Alexander, P. (2001) 'Difference – A Way Forward?' *TA UK*, No. 60, 21–3.

Bimrose, J. & Bayne R. (1995) 'A Multicultural Framework in Counsellor Training: A Preliminary Evaluation. *British Journal of Guidance and Counselling*, 23(2), 259.

Cocks, G. (1997) *Psychotherapy in the Third Reich: The Göring Institute* (second edition). New Brunswick, NJ: Transaction Publishers.

Corker, M. (1994) *The Deaf Challenge*. London: Jessica Kingsley.

Cropper, A. & Burke, B. (2000) 'Is Higher Education Good for your Health? – Black Students' Experiences in Social Work Education', in *Proceedings of the International Social Work Conference on Multiculturalism in Social Work and Mental Health Practice*. New York University.

Costello, J., Roy, B. & Steiner, C. (1988) 'Competition', in B. Roy & C. Steiner (eds), *Radical Psychiatry: The Second Decade*. Unpublished manuscript, 55–67.

Dalrymple J. & Burke B. (1995) *Anti-oppressive Practice – Social Care and the Law*. Buckingham: Open University Press.

Freire, P. (1972) *The Pedagogy of the Oppressed* (M.B. Ramos, trans.) Harmondsworth: Penguin.

French, S. (1996) 'Simulation Exercises in Disability Awareness Training: A Critique', in G. Hales (ed.), *Beyond Disability*. London. Sage, 114–23.

Glen, M. (1971) 'On Training Therapists', in J. Agel (ed.), *The Radical Therapist*. New York: Ballantine Books, 8–17.

Gurnah, A. (1984) 'The Politics of Racism Awareness Training'. *Critical Social Policy*?, 6–20.

Jones, J.M. (1972) *Prejudice and Racism*. Reading, MA: Addison-Wesley.

Kearney, A. (1996) *Counselling, Class and Politics: Undeclared Influences in Therapy*. Manchester: PCCS Books.

Natiello, P. (1987) 'The Person-centered Approach: From Theory to Practice.' *Person-Centered Review*, 2, 203–16.

Natiello, P. (1990) 'The Person-centered Approach, Collaborative Power, and Cultural Transformation'. *Person-Centered Review*, 5(3), 268–86.

O'Connor, N. & Ryan, J. (1993) *Wild Desires and Mistaken Identities: Lesbianism and Psychoanalysis*. New York: Columbia University Press.

Ridley, C. (1995) *Overcoming Unintentional Racism in Counseling and Therapy – A Practitioners' Guide to Intentional Intervention*. London: Sage.

Robertson, C. (1993) 'Dysfunction in Training Organisations'. *Self and Society*, 21(4), 31–5.

Rogers, C.R. (1951) *Client-centered Therapy*. London: Constable.

Rogers, C.R. (1978) *Carl Rogers on Personal Power*. London: Constable.

Samuels A. (2001) 'Politics on the Couch'. *Counselling and Psychotherapy Journal*, 12(1), BACP.

Schwartz, J. (1999) *Cassandra's Daughter: A History of Psychoanalysis*. London: Penguin.

Sivanandan, A. (1985) 'RAT and the degradation of black struggle', *Race & Class*, XXXVI(4), 1–33.

Smith, B. (1996) *A Study into the Attitudes of Counselling Students Towards Marginalised Groups*. Unpublished MA dissertation: Liverpool UK.

Steiner, C. (1984) 'Emotional Literacy'. *Transactional Analysis Journal*, 14(3), 162–73.

Taylor-Muhammad, F. (2001) 'Follow Fashion Monkey Never Drink Good Soup: Black Counsellors and the Road to Inclusion'. *Counselling and Psychotherapy Journal*, 12(6), 10–13.

Thompson, N. (1997) *Anti-Discriminatory Practice*. London: Macmillan.

Thompson, N. (1998) *Promoting Equality: Challenging Discrimination and Oppression in the Human Services*. London. Macmillan.

Tudor, K. (1999) '"I'm OK, You're OK – and They're OK": Therapeutic Relationships in Transactional Analysis', in C. Feltham (ed.), *Understanding the Counselling Relationship*. London: Sage, 90–119.

Wheeler, S. (1996) *Training Counsellors: The Assessment of Competence*. London: Cassell.

Wilson, A. & Beresford, P. (2000) 'Anti-Oppressive Practice: Emancipation or Appropriation'. *British Journal of Social Work*, 30, 553–73.

Wood, J. (1990) 'Children Discover how it Feels to be Disabled'. *Therapy Weekly*, 16(40), 10.

Index

abortion, 101, 104–5
access to counselling, physical
        barriers to, 42
'acting out' behaviour, 77–8
activity theory, 91
age affirmative practice, 95–6
age of consent, 53, 82
ageism, 87–91
        institutional, 89
        internalized, 89
Aleman, S., 121
Alexander, P., 147
Althusser, L., 5
American Psychiatric Association, 125
anti-disablist practice, 42–3
anti-discriminatory practice, 1–4, 35,
        47, 84, 140
anti-oppressive practice, 1–4,
        10–12, 74, 82–4, 107, 128,
        131, 137–9, 145, 148
antipsychiatry, 68–9
anti-racism, 16, 24–9
Association for Christian
        Counsellors, 136
attachment behaviour, 90
awareness training, 137

Baker-Miller, J., 63
Banks, N., 81
Barnes, C., 37
Bayne, R., 136
Bennet, A., 93
Beresford, P., 10–11, 128, 146
Berger, P.L., 5
Bernstein, B., 115
Bimrose, J., 136
black clients for counselling, 16, 93
Black Identity Model, 22–4
black therapists, 81

Blakemore, K., 121–2
Blumenfeld, W.J., 52
Boneham, M., 121–2
Bowlby, J., 90, 96
Boyd-Franklyn, N., 101
British Association for Counselling
        and Psychotherapy, 1, 16, 128
Brown, L., 72
bullying, 55, 81–2
Burke, B., 1, 144, 147
Burstow, B., 4, 9–10

Campaign Against Living Miserably
        (CALM), 77
capital, ownership of, 109–10
Carter, R.T., 6–7
Cass, C., 93
Chaplin, J., 66
Child and Adolescent Mental Health
        Services, 77
child-centred counselling, 75–86
child disability, 83–4
child sexual abuse, 72–3
Children's Fund, 77
class consciousness, 109
        social differences, 84–5, 95, 109–16
'class-blindness', 114
'colour blindness', 21, 25, 109
contracting, 78
Copernicus, Nicolaus, 96
Corker, M., 123, 146
countertransference, 57, 130
Coyle, A., 123
Cropper, A., 147
Cross, M., 38
Crouan, M., 123
cultural values, 25–7
culture and religion, 101–3
cyber counselling, 10

Dalal, F., 125
Dalrymple, J., 1, 144
D'Augelli, A.R., 82–3
Davies, D., 51–2
Davis, K., 33–4
deficit models of clientele, 116
dementia, 84–5
Denneny, M., 52–3, 58
dependency, 40, 89
depersonalization, 9
disability, 33–4, 94
    in children, 83–4
    social and medical models
        of, 35–7, 46
disability awareness training, 43, 137
Disability Discrimination Act (1995), 33, 37
disabling identity, 40–1
disabling practice, 37
discourse analysis, 5–6
discrimination, 1–3, 7, 121–2
    against disabled people, 33
disengagement theory, 90–1
Docker-Drysdale, B., 77
Dominelli, L., 17, 109

early years initiatives, 77
eating disorders, 73–4
emotional literacy, 77
empathy, *political*, 70–1
equal opportunities training, 137
Erikson, E., 96
Erkis, A.J., 125
Ethnic Identity Development
        models, 20–4
exclusion, 9
exploitation, 139
external locus of control and of
        responsibility, 106
externalization in counselling, 29

Featherstone, M., 89
Feltham, C., 1
feminism, 62, 67
Fernando, S., 127
Finkelstein, V., 83–4
Franklin, A.J., 6
Freire, Paulo, 136, 146

French, S., 137
Freud, Sigmund, 39, 87–8, 96,
        99–100, 125, 142

Gandhi, Mohandas, 96
gay affirmative practice, 50–3, 57–9
Gergen, K., 43
Giddins, A., 109
Glen, M., 135
Greenspan, M., 70
Grey Panthers movement, 96

Hall, S., 5
Hargaden, H., 115
Havighurst, R.J., 90–1
Hayes, J.A., 125
hegemony, 5
Helms, Janet, 128
Herman, J., 72
hierarchical relationships and hierarchical
        thinking, 65–7
Hirst, J., 76
Hitchens, Christopher, 2
HIV, 53
homophobia, 51–8, 82–3, 123, 144, 147
homosexuality, 50–4, 94, 125, 136
    counsellors' responses to, 55–8
hooks, bell, 25–6
Horton, I., 1
Hutchinson, M.G., 63
Hutchinson Encyclopaedia, 5
Hutton, Will, 8

identities
    disabling, 40–1
    formation of, 20
    multiple, 120–2, 126–8
    racial, 7, 81
ideology, 38
    definition of, 4–5
    and hegemony, 5
impairment as distinct from
        disability, 35–6
individualism, 139
Institute for the Healing of Racism, 4
internal locus of control and of
        responsibility, 106

internalization, 5
  of ageism, 89–90
  of disability, 84
  of homophobia, 52, 57–8
  of racism, 18–19, 28
International Psychoanalytic
  Association, 136
International Year of Older Persons
  (1999), 96
Irigaray, L., 125

Jacobs, M., 99–100
jargon, 9
Jenness, L., 121
Jones, J.M., 140
Jung, Carl, 125

Katz, J., 27
Kaye, J., 43
Kearney, A., 123
knowledge, social construction of, 112
Kuhn, Maggie, 96
Kuper, A., 124

Lacan, J., 39, 125
Lago, C., 127
Laing, R.D., 3
language, use of, 8–10, 38, 148
Lawrence, Stephen, 16–17
learning environments, 145–9
Lee, C.C., 10
lesbians, gays and bisexuals
  (LGB), 82–3
Lewis, T., 72
life books, 81
Lines, D., 82
Lobel, K., 72
Lorde, A., 122
loss, theories of, 45
Luthar, S.S., 121

McLeod, J., 39, 43
Macpherson Report (1999), 17
Mandela, Nelson, 4
manual and non-manual work, 110–11
marginalized groups, 7, 126
Marx, Karl, 109–10

masculinization of counselling, 63–4
Maylon, A., 50
medical services, 114–15
Meir, Golda, 96
mentoring, 147
middle class attitudes, values
  and language, 110–16
Moodley, R., 128
mothering, 64–5, 96
multiculturalism, 24, 124, 147
multiple (cultural) jeopardy,
  121–2, 129–31
multiple oppressions, 92–5

Natiello, P., 138
National (UK) Health Service, 88, 95
National (US) Urban League, 121
Neal, C., 51
Norman, Alison, 121

older people, counselling of, 87–97
Oliver, M., 37
ontogenesis, stages of, 96
oppression, 1–4, 7, 109, 113–14, 136, 139
  levels of, 140–1
Orbach, S., 73
Oswin, M., 38
otherness, 7, 63, 122–3

patriarchy, 62–6, 72
Paz, J., 121
Pederson, P.B., 99–100
pensioners, 95
person-centred counselling, 146
Philadelphia (film), 145
Pink Therapy books, 50
political correctness, 8
postmodernism, 122, 142
poverty, 117

racial identity, 7, 81
racism, 16–24 *passim*, 79–81, 109, 123, 140
  cultural, 25–8
  institutional, 17, 80
  internalized, 18–19, 28
  unconscious, 93
radical feminist therapy, 68–72

Ratna, Hillary, 45
Raymond, D., 52
reflexive practice, 105–7
Registrar General's social class
    categorization, 110
religious orientation, 99–107
reminiscence therapy, 91
resilience factors, 79–80
rhythmic approach to understanding
    change, 64–6
Ridley, C., 135
'risk and resilience' framework, 84–5
Rivers, I., 55
Rochlin, M., 7
Rogers, Carl, 138, 142–4
root metaphors, 39, 47

Samuels, A., 144
Sashidharan, S., 124
Scrutton, S., 89, 95
Section 28 (of Local Government Act
    1988), 52–3, 82
self, sense of, 54, 56, 59
sexist scripts, 71
sexuality
    of older people, 91–2
    of young people, 82–3
shadism, 20, 23
Shrof, F.M., 63
Sikhism, 102–4
simulation exercises, 137
smacking of children, 75–6
Smith, B., 78, 85, 135
social class *see* class
social context, 4
social justice, 26
social work, 2–3, 10–11, 109
socialization, 66, 84
special schools, 84
Spender, D., 9
spirituality, 99
Steiner, C., 78
stereotyping, 9, 35–9, 123–4, 137
Sterne, D.N., 115

stigma, 9
Stirling, E., 94
Stuart, O., 83–4
SubCo Elders Day Centre, 93
Sue, D.W. and D., 20, 106, 127
suicide, 55–6, 77, 82–3
Summers, G., 115
Szasz, Thomas, 3

Taylor-Muhammad, F., 142
theory and practice, integration of, 143–5
Thompson, J., 127
Thompson, N., 1–5, 8–9, 140
training of counsellors, 111–13, 135–49
transference, 57, 130
turbans, wearing of, 102–3

'underclass' phenomenon, 110
unemployment, 111
United Nations Convention on the Rights
    of the Child, 76

violence, 62–3, 70

Walker, Alice: *The Color Purple*, 145
Weber, Max, 110
Wernick, A., 89
Whalen, M., 74
Wheeler, S., 143
White Identity Model, 20–2
Widdowson, M., 79
Wilson, A., 10–11, 128, 146
Winnicott, D.W., 96, 128
Withers, S., 40–1
woman-centred practice, 62–7, 69
Wood, J., 137
world views, 106
Worthington, E.L., 100, 103
Wyckoff, Hogie, 68

YAVIS effect, 125

Zera, D., 93
Zoja, L., 92